T0210038

Praise for At The Helm

"Thank you for the simplicity of your book. Although the concepts are deep and profound, you captured them in a way that anyone can understand and utilize. The way you wove your own personal stories throughout the book is probably what I liked the most. It humanizes the concepts and brings them to life."

Mia Jerritt,
Executive & Integrated Life Coaching

"This book is an inspiring true story of the author's personal transformation. In it, Michael offers you a practical and proven step-by-step approach that will make it easy for you to embrace the necessary changes required to step into action and transform your health, your career, and your relationships—beginning with yourself."

Maureen (Mo) Hagan, Canadian Fitness Influencer,
Entrepreneur, Author and Speaker

"Michael is honestly one of the best souls I know. His advice is the real deal. I was truly inspired to watch his personal transformation over the years from a corporate-type guy to becoming an expert in health, wellness and personal development. Now his book, **At the Helm**, provides you with a practical framework to make your own transformation to a life of clarity and joy."

Jimmie Inch, Entrepreneur,
Structural Engineer, Musician, TV Host & Business Coach

AT THE HELM

living your life with more
clarity, fulfillment and joy

michael doyle

BALBOA.PRESS
A DIVISION OF HAY HOUSE

Balboa Press books may be ordered through booksellers or by contacting:

Balboa Press
A Division of Hay House
1663 Liberty Drive
Bloomington, IN 47403
www.balboapress.com
844-682-1282

Because of the dynamic nature of the Internet, any web addresses or
links contained in this book may have changed since publication and may
no longer be valid. The views expressed in this work are solely those
of the author and do not necessarily reflect the views of the publisher,
and the publisher hereby disclaims any responsibility for them.

The author of this book does not dispense medical advice or prescribe the use
of any technique as a form of treatment for physical, emotional, or medical
problems without the advice of a physician, either directly or indirectly. The
intent of the author is only to offer information of a general nature to help
you in your quest for emotional and spiritual well-being. In the event you use
any of the information in this book for yourself, which is your constitutional
right, the author and the publisher assume no responsibility for your actions.

Any people depicted in stock imagery provided by Getty Images are
models, and such images are being used for illustrative purposes only.
Certain stock imagery © Getty Images.

Cover Design by Carolyn McNall

Print information available on the last page.

ISBN: 978-1-9822-7914-1 (sc)
ISBN: 978-1-9822-7915-8 (e)

Balboa Press rev. date: 01/20/2023

This book is dedicated to my parents Patrick and Mary Doyle.

From my earliest childhood memories to my life today, I can honestly say you have always been there for me. Your caring, understanding and loving ways are just a part of who you are. It didn't matter if I was running my company up North, working for the government, going back to school at age 35, or launching my coaching company — your belief in me always shines through. I am so grateful for all the loving memories and I look forward to the many great times ahead.

I love you both with all my heart.
Thank you!

CONTENTS

INTRODUCTION

We are all on a journey in life, searching for purpose, happiness and love. At times, we are glowing and at other times, we may feel dim, but the process of healing, forgiving and growing is an amazing experience.

Sometimes we have to hit rock bottom in order to produce an urgency to make a change, but we are indeed *At the Helm* of our own ship and ultimately responsible for the life we live. Living fully is a choice, just like living an *average* or even *unhappy* life is a choice. I encourage you to live fully.

As I share my stories and my lessons on these pages, you will see that I too have been at the bottom and struggled to pull myself up. But it is my full belief that each of us can do amazing things in life when we believe we can and when our passion is ignited. I know you can do it, regardless of whatever your early circumstances might have been or what current situation you're in now.

Like most people, I have had great times in my life but also great struggles. But now I feel so much more in control of my life, it has been an amazing transformation. I went from being unhealthy and way overweight, feeling depressed and disappointed with myself, to a place now where I am productive, happy and passionate about my life and my future. I'd like to tell you just a little about my life this far and then I will introduce to you the process of personal transformation that worked so well for me and for others whom I am working with now.

Growing up with Family and Music

I was blessed with a great childhood and upbringing, growing up in a modest house in Northern Bay, Newfoundland. My mother and father are loving, honest and hardworking. They are always there for me especially when I need them the most.

In our family, there were four children, two boys and two girls. My brother Patrick is the youngest, then there was me, and we had two older sisters, Darlene and Sharon. Unfortunately, more than 30 years ago, we lost our sister Darlene in a terrible car accident. Darlene and her friend Karen were hit and killed by a drunk driver. You never fully get over something like that, but our family grew even stronger. We moved forward knowing that Darlene would always be with us in our hearts and in spirit.

From my earliest memories, there was always music in the house. When I was about 12 years old, I started playing guitar and I quickly became very passionate about music. I released my first album in 1996, and our band was thrilled when tracks from our CD were later included on several compilations with other famous groups such as *The Irish Rovers* and *Great Big Sea*. I still love to gig with the guys from one of my later bands, *The Northern*

Ramblers, when I can. We had all kinds of experiences in our travels, even being nominated for DVD of the Year at the East Coast Music Awards.

But it was actually a trip to the Arctic that took me from Newfoundland to Iqaluit in the first place. I was visiting my brother and sister there and I soon found it was an incredible place to live and work. Initially, I worked a maintenance job for Nunastar Properties. I also ran a bookkeeping company for several years and then went on to work for the Federal Government as a Financial Analyst for more than 13 years.

I loved that job because people from across the region came to me for all kinds of help and advice, not just financial. I think it was because I'm good at seeing the big picture and making decisions with very little stress in the process.

In my free time, I ensured I fueled my passionate for music and entrepreneurship. That's how I managed to perform on, engineer, or produce more than 20 albums over the years, several of them while I was living up North. I also established and ran a successful live sound studio and recording company called *Doyle Entertainment Inc.* That was a great growing experience for me because I got to set up and run live sound for a number of fabulous music and arts festivals.

While my love and talent for music has been a blessing, the lifestyle that came along with it for many years wasn't very good. Too many times, I found myself waking up the next morning after a great gig and a fun night, but I was so completely hung over from too much drinking that sometimes I could hardly remember how I got home. After one really bad night, which you'll hear more about in the next chapter, I clearly had reached a point where I knew things had to change. I was finally sick of being sick, and knew I had to do something about it.

Fortunately, I had a very supportive environment which helped me overcome many obstacles and I was able to take it one day at a time. Through a series of small steps, I could feel a snowball effect of positive change happening which gave me the momentum to keep up with my new habits. I was still scared about being able to do it, but the person I was becoming was able to manage my fear in a powerful way. As I write this today, it's been more than a decade since I've had a drink, my body is fit, healthy, and my life is more fulfilling in every way.

At the Helm of Your Own Ship

I have read that life begins at the end of your comfort zone and this has proven to be true in my life. Even when I was busy night and day in Iqaluit, and always expanding my personal horizons, I knew in the back of my mind that I was meant to do a lot *more*. That's why when I relocated with Molly and our son Timothy to Ontario in 2015, I took that move as a sign that it was time to follow my heart. Although shortly after our marriage ended for the greater good of all involved, that move proved to be the catalyst for much expansion along my divine journey.

Once my mind was clear, I continued exploring my interests in personal development, human potential, and peak performance as well as learning more about fitness and nutrition. Over the years, this knowledge served to open my mind up to the power that I had over my own destiny. Once I experienced how good life can be, I realized that I'd really like to become a personal and business coach. That way I could do one-on-one mentoring to help other people bring out their own potential. I also enjoy being on stage, in front of large and small groups, so I started doing more inspirational speaking and training on these topics.

I called this new business venture *Doyle It In*, and every day since I started it, I've been energized to keep reaching out to more and more people with my message. What I bring is a common sense approach that anyone can use to improve their life. When I show people how they can link up the many key areas of their lives and make a series of small changes, they too realize their dreams are within their control, which is an incredible feeling.

While organizing the ideas for my workshops, I clearly saw that my concepts break out into five main sections, which I call pillars. These five pillars provide a practical framework that sets the stage for powerful and sustainable life changes. I've structured the book and my workshops around the following pillars because I find this is an easy way for other people to grasp and implement the process:

- Core desires and setting intention.
- Removing obstacles and limiting beliefs.
- Developing a positive mindset.
- Building a solid foundation.
- Taking effective action.

Right now, you may be struggling with your life in any number of ways or know someone who is. I felt called to share my experiences so I could hopefully inspire others to make positive changes for themselves. I know if I could do it, so can anyone else. It just starts with assessing where you are in your life now and deciding where you want to improve. Then you set your intention and continue to follow the rest of the pillars to success.

This whole process of change starts with gaining clarity, but before jumping into that, I just want to say that your health has to be at the top of your priority list. Healthy eating, combined with a suitable fitness plan and an active lifestyle, will give you the energy, mental clarity and confidence to move forward with passion and purpose.

I know firsthand that if you don't have your health, you can't help yourself or serve others in a sustainable and meaningful way. That's why I've included my personal recommendations on nutrition and fitness at the end of this book in the Valuable Resources sections # 1 and # 2. These are useful general tips that I often give to clients so they can begin to develop and maintain the habits required to reach and maintain a healthy lifestyle.

How to Use this Book

Now it's time to dive in and *Doyle It In* yourself. In each chapter, I'll share stories and insights to help you learn more about each pillar, which are the main steps in the process. To really drive home, the concepts, I've included a few practical exercises at the end of each chapter to help you apply these concepts to your daily life. I encourage you to do your best to engage with the exercises and try them out.

Each time you make a change to your daily routine, even a small one, you'll see that you do have the power to change your life. Each step you take builds momentum and I feel confident that you will experience a big impact over time. Each moment that you experience personal growth, you become a better version of your former self. And since it all starts with clarity, that's where we are going first. Just turn the page and get ready to transform your life toward a better and brighter future.

PILLAR
1

Core Desires and Setting Intention

PILLAR 1

Core Desires and
Setting Intention

Waking up one morning in my mid-30s, groggy, sick and exhausted, I realized that I couldn't keep going on that way. My son was calling to me to play with him, but I was overweight by more than 60 pounds, not eating healthy at all, and drinking too much just about every night. My drinking habits were affecting not only my personal health but too many aspects of my life. Fortunately, that morning on April 2010, it was like a light came on. I knew it was time to make some major changes.

I couldn't help but contemplate how my life had spun out of control to this degree. I recalled that I had played a show the night before with the band but I couldn't remember singing the last set or how I even got home. I had to admit to myself that this kind of thing was happening a lot more often than before and it scared me to think about what I had to lose if I kept on this same destructive path.

So as I sat trying to play with my son Timothy who was 14- months-old that next morning, with my head pounding, I decided to take control of my life. Here was my beautiful son who was so innocent and all he wanted was to play with his Dad. I needed to shape up so I would have the energy to give him the life I really wanted him to have. I wanted to be active and engaged and be able to teach him all the things a father should. It had always been one of my core desires, to be the best father and family man I could possibly be, and there I was completely sick and exhausted at 8 in the morning.

I'll admit this wasn't the first time I had decided to quit drinking. But it was the first time I felt 100% committed.

Looking into my son's shining eyes, my *why* for making a change was bigger than my usual *excuses* for not doing so. I simply couldn't continue with my hard-living lifestyle, so that day I asked for help from a higher power and somehow surrendered the struggle on a deeper level.

I had no idea how much that decision would affect me. I didn't even really know where to begin so I just took a small step at first. The next morning, I started walking to work each day. Imagine my surprise when within the first few months, I had lost more than 20 pounds. By adding a little activity and no longer drinking, I could see that my health was improving and heading in a positive direction. Plus, I had a lot more time for my family, which felt fantastic.

Once I started to feel the momentum building, I felt motivated to clean up my nutritional habits, so I started eating breakfast again. As I continued making small changes over time, I found myself becoming more in tune with what my body needed. We all have the power to make small daily changes, creating positive improvements in our lives and on the people around us.

With my new found energy that summer, while on vacation in Newfoundland I went to a running track with Molly and my sister Sharon. They had both been runners before but I had never been on a running track. Molly walked with me and asked if I wanted to run for a little while. My initial thought was not really all that enthusiastic: *Why don't you just kick me in the stomach instead and call it a day?*

Then I thought again, and it occurred to me that there was no harm in trying. I started running a bit, then walking, and kept repeating that over and over, until several laps had passed. I realized that I actually liked the feeling when I was running and I ran at the track every day that week, starting to enjoy the groove.

Once I was back in Iqaluit after that vacation, I kept on running. When I mentioned to a friend at work that I was starting to run a lot more, he suggested I should maybe run with another colleague of ours named Paul Fraser so I could keep myself more motivated and accountable.

When I heard this, I was apprehensive to say the least. After all, one of my mottos had always been, *if it's not broke, don't fix it.* At the time, I was enjoying my solo running routine. Plus, Paul had run many marathons and half marathons in the past and was once again training for another event. I had no idea if he would take on someone new like me, so I thought about it for a while before speaking to him.

But when I did ask Paul about it, he was great and said sure, we could run two mornings a week together if I wanted. And later on, after we became pretty regular running buddies, he admitted that he too had felt the same way when he started out, agreeing that it can be really beneficial to have a running partner for support and encouragement. We went on to become great friends during my time in Iqaluit. Paul and his son went on to encourage me even further in my fitness journey and my personal goals, something I am totally grateful for. But more about that in the next chapter!

For now, just let me say that once I started losing weight, it was mostly from cardiovascular exercise. But once I was introduced to strength training with the help of an awesome personal trainer, I added that to my regime and loved that feeling too, becoming stronger by the day. Not building bulk but muscle, and I added it to my routine to stay in the best overall shape I could.

I wondered what to explore next, because by that time, I felt I had gone as far as I could with my fitness and nutritional knowledge base. Still I felt called to keep learning, and I was happy when I found a 12-month online coaching program for men by Precision Nutrition that seemed to meet my needs. I learned a tremendous amount about nutrition and fitness, which enabled me to continue to transform my body, my focus and my life.

Six months into that program, I was feeling so good every day, with a full handle on my nutritional needs and having more than enough energy to keep up with work, family, live music events, and music production. It was to the point that when I thought about leaving the North so we could be closer to family, that the advertisements for finance jobs just didn't appeal to me anymore. Instead, I thought about getting some certifications of my own in fitness while still working in finance and working out the details about the move.

I was able to do some of that new training through the same company that was offering the online men's program that I was taking so it worked out great. Over the next six months or so, I earned my canfitpro Personal Trainer Specialist certification, plus certifications in functional movement screening, and ISSA fitness training.

So overall, within about 14 months, I had quit drinking and started to really clean up my diet and exercise habits.

I took up walking first and then running. I lost 65 pounds and completed two sprint triathlons. But it all started with becoming very clear on my core desires and setting a definite intention: *I wanted to be a good dad, a positive role model and I wanted to be 100% there for my family.* Once I committed to work at cleaning up my daily routines, I just took one small step at a time, one day at a time, and I was amazed how it completely transformed my life.

Taking Your First Steps to Clarity

I love Pillar One because it is about becoming clear on your core desires and setting intention. Although it can take a while to get moving in the right direction, there is so much clarity, growth and momentum that will follow! When I look back on my life, I can see that I was guilty of not taking time to become clear on my core desires. I was scared of it because it meant looking *inward*, inside myself, for that clarity. I know first-hand that doing this kind of inner work can be scary and uncomfortable. Believe me, *I totally get it.*

But the benefits are worth it. You're already a good person but any positive feelings about yourself might be mired under the muck of fear and insecurity the way it was for me for many years. The truth is that all too often we don't give ourselves enough credit for things we have successfully done in our lives. Even in my 20s and early 30s, I had actually accomplished quite a bit in my career in finance and with my music, but eventually it was overshadowed by my drinking and the depressing thoughts I had about my weight and the direction my life was heading at that time.

Now that I have far more clarity, I can now feel proud of my personal achievements. I have grown, even while writing this book, to the point where I can confidently and comfortably say *I am good* at something. In fact, I am great at a lot of things and I am excited now to be able to show other people how they can create greater value for themselves each day and improve their lives. I also believe strongly that we can all learn from others along the way. Life is about the journey, and how we can serve others while living fully.

In a relatively short period of time, you too can start to feel your momentum building and experience the tremendous benefits of becoming clear on your core desires and setting *powerful intentions*.

There is an equation I share with clients which sums up this process quite well. You may have seen something similar before; many inspirational leaders suggest similar principles. The equation I use takes three personal elements—thought, passion and action—and states that when you add them together, you get powerful outcomes.

Thought + Passion + Action = Powerful Outcomes

Looking Inside Yourself

When you take the time to go inward and dig a little deeper into your core desires, that's when you really start to transform as a person. There are many ways to accomplish this, and I'm very happy to share three powerful exercises at the end of this chapter that I feel work really well for most people.

There are many useful techniques for developing a clear vision of your core desires. Personally, I feel that creating a vision board is a powerful first step that anyone can do. I t's extremely effective especially when you follow it up with other actions that move you toward making your vision a reality. The first *Doyle It In* exercise walks y o u t h rough t h is process which is a fun way to get started. After that, you'll find a series of questions that will prompt you to think more about what makes you excited about life, getting you to start exploring your passions and desires. The third exercise walks you through a process of setting initial intentions that tie in with your core desires.

Once you start to discover what makes you tick and you begin to formulate your first statements of intention, I highly recommend that you begin making some positive changes right away, even if they are just small things at first. Of course, you may still continue to do more clarity work in the future, but don't delay taking action now because you're not yet *crystal clear* or *completely clear* on everything in your life. Just start somewhere. Do what you can in any area in order to get going. Any step in the right direction is positive progress.

This worked incredibly well for me, just jumping in and getting something going. For me it was my initial decision to walk to work. That act of *walking to work* wasn't going to solve all my health problems, personal fears or nagging concerns overnight, but it was a step I felt I *could* do. I had a lot more stuff going on with trying to quit drinking and put my home life back on track and still keep up with all my commitments, but rather than be paralyzed by trying to resolve it all at once, I just took one simple step. I said I would start walking to work and *I did*. And that made all the difference.

Seeking Inspiration from All Kinds of Sources

In addition to trying the exercises in this chapter to help you with clarity, intention and initial goal setting, I also encourage you to seek out various kinds of resources to see what sits best with you. When I was exploring many different personal development courses, I found that one of my favorite ones was working with Christine Kane from North Carolina. She is an inspirational speaker and trainer who helps entrepreneurs achieve greater levels of success in their businesses and in life.

I was particularly inspired by what she teaches about *intention* and personal power. I took several programs and courses with her that really helped me gain clarity on the direction of my business. I feel each of us should try to grow personally each day, in some way. It's about becoming the person you need to be to do the things you want to do.

When you find a development program, course or leader that clicks with you, I encourage you to dig in, learn the principles, and then do the daily work to make the changes you desire. Many resources from these leaders are free online (including on my own website) so you can get started anytime. Looking for the right kind of inspirational messages for you is yet another small step that will help keep you motivated as you continue to take action and build up to bigger cumulative results over time.

Setting Intentions that Work

The next natural progression once you have increased your inner clarity is goal setting with intention. This enables you to ignite your *why* and work towards the life you seek. Your first goals might be quite simple and just deal with one current pressing situation, but eventually as you grow and move forward, you will set goals with even more powerful intentions. Again it's natural for your goals at first to be smaller in nature and evolve over time into bigger kinds of things.

Eventually you will create a purpose-driven life which is an amazing way of being. When you reach that mark, you'll start each day with purpose and with powerful intention. But at first you don't need to know all the answers and how you are going to take the next 5, 10 or 20 steps. Just remain positive and determined as you proceed and that will carry you well in the beginning.

In my experience, intention does evolve over time to what it is ultimately meant to be. It doesn't matter what your initial new goals are as long as they are in alignment with who you are inside. And be aware that any true core desire goal you set will be win-win and it will not harm anyone else in the process.

Another lesson I learned from Christine Kane was about two types of intention. One is *intention from* and the other is *intention to*. I didn't realize it at the time but my intention when moving from my career in finance toward my new career as a personal trainer involved my *intention from*. It would get me out from one career path that no longer worked for me, so I could begin working to help others. The fact that I am super passionate about nutrition and fitness made it exciting as well.

However, once I gave up my desk job and entered the personal training field, I quickly found out that it was just the tip of the iceberg in terms of how I wanted to positively impact other people's lives. I decided I actually wanted to become a personal and business coach, motivational speaker, and author so I could eventually help others on a global scale. I have a story as we all do and I'm happy to tell my story, put myself out there, and help as many people as I can. As often happens, my life has become more than an *intention from*. It is now an *intention to … to give, to inspire, and to transform.*

Now it's *Your Turn to Doyle It In* and start to take your own first steps in your process. Some of the questions and suggestions may be a bit uncomfortable or stir up your insides, but I encourage you to take a deep breath and do your best. Your answers or actions don't have to be perfect or comprehensive at this point, just get started. You can always come back later and repeat any of these steps or exercises whenever you want. That's the beauty of doing this personal work: any positive step you take today is better than doing nothing.

Doyle It In Exercise #1:

Create Your Own Vision Board

You may know what a vision board is or you may not. Not that long ago, I had no idea what this was, but now I realize that millions of people around the world have used this technique or some variation of it to help themselves develop clarity and get in touch with their core desires. I was excited when I discovered how easy it was to create my own vision board and the power it holds.

The steps to making a vision board are quite straightforward and cost virtually nothing. Find yourself a large piece of paper, poster board or cardboard to start with. Gather some old magazines, brochures or anything with colorful photos and words on it, and get a pair of scissors. Begin by flipping through the materials and pull out any kinds of images, words or phrases that speak to you and inspire you. Don't over think it, just select whatever you like. *Go with your gut.*

You can select images of things, people, experiences, places, or phrases that you'd like to have in your life, or have more of in your life. Once you have a pile of images torn out, then sort through them and choose the ones you really love. Trim around those images and then arrange them on the larger poster board or paper in any way you like, overlapping them like a montage or put them in a grid or whatever looks best to you.

Once you like the layout, stick the images down with glue or tape. You can add any extra words that you like with a marker, or even add a photo of yourself. Find a spot in your home or at the office where you can put this poster up on the wall, in a place where you will see it each day, and you're done! It's that easy. I have yet to meet anyone who can't accomplish this. There are no wrong ways to do it. Whatever you create is *yours.*

The vision board process encourages you to take time to really think about the life you want, including who and what you want in your life. If you put the time and effort into this process, you can't help but become "clear" on what you want. It just naturally brings out your core desires. That's why vision boards are so powerful and why they are extremely effective, especially when followed up with appropriate actions toward making those ideas a reality.

A vision board increases clarity and helps you visualize, for this reason I am a believer. The funny thing is that I had created a poster like this during the time I was taking the 12-month online men's coaching program, but didn't know what it was called at the time. I used a large piece of construction paper and put it up in the back of my closet where I saw it each day. On it, I stuck all different images, including progress photos of myself taken over time, as my body started getting into better shape. I included a picture of someone with a similar body type to me but in *elite condition* so I would have something to work toward. I put inspirational sayings on it to keep me motivated and list of short term goals that I highlighted in blue when I completed them.

What I created back then was a simple version of this vision board concept and it helped me focus just on one single area of my life, namely my *fitness goals*. It turned out to be a very effective visual daily reminder about that one area of my life. What I am suggesting for you is that you create more of a true vision board which encompasses all areas of your life, serving as a holistic snapshot of your dreams, desires and intentions. Make yours not just about a specific goal but an overview of all the good things you want to manifest in your life.

Within the last year, I made a true vision board and it included a sketch of this book with positive thoughts around it, like *More than 2 million Sold, Best Seller* and so on. My board also had sections on family, love, nutrition, music, and fitness which are all deep passions of mine. I also put images on my board about mindset and the power of believing.

In the center I put a picture of me in a sea kayak next to an iceberg that was more than a hundred feet in length. I chose this picture because the look on my face clearly illustrates I am feeling pure "joy" and truly alive. I couldn't resist so I also put a photo of a '69 Camaro and I wrote *Financial Freedom* above the picture. You may notice as you read on in this book that just about every topic in the Five Pillars and in my Valuable Resources pages was reflected on my vision board, even before those Pillars were fully developed the way they are here.

Doyle It In Exercise #2:

Become Clear on Your Core Desires

Another great way to discover your core desires is to think about what you are passionate about. I find the following questions are a solid way to get your mind moving in this direction. Just take out a pen and paper, a journal that you like, or bring up your computer screen and record the most honest answers you can to the following questions.

- Can you think of a time when you were just totally full of joy and energy? If so, what were you doing in that moment? In other words, what floats your boat?
- What are you truly passionate about? If you're not sure, that's OK and it's actually very common. Clarity comes with time and patience. So if you prefer, just list a few of your favorite hobbies instead.
- What do people tell you you're great at doing?
- What would you say are your main strengths?
- If money wasn't an issue, what would you work at?

- What level of overall health, fitness, and energy would you like to have?
- Look at your life 3 to 5 years in the future and describe where would you like to live and in what kind of home? And who will be there with you? How will you pass your time? Think about why you'd love this life.

If you feel any resistance about answering these questions, that's OK. Try taking a deep breath or two or three. Now try asking yourself, "Why am I not ready to dig deeper and write these answers up right now? *Why am I hesitating?*" See what comes up for you, and just make note of it. As you move through the rest of the exercises and Pillars in this book, I expect you'll start to understand more about yourself and what's holding you back. You can always come back to this exercise at any time.

Doyle It In Exercise #3:

Set Your Initial Intentions

Now that you've taken the time to get clear on your core desires, it's important to set an intention that is in alignment with your core beliefs and who you are. This is an awesome starting point for achieving any goal because when you set a clear intention, your inner power is naturally activated.

But I just want to remind you again not to become discouraged if the clarity is not there yet. I find with clients that the goals that they set initially at this point will change over time, and those goals will evolve over time into the meaningful path the person is meant to take. At this point, just know that any positive goal is a step in the right direction.

Think about your core desires, and then beside each prompt below, just write down what comes from your heart. Make each goal something you feel is attainable, not impossible. Then try to formulate an intention statement to get you started toward that particular goal.

In my case, I might have written my first goal as, "Get moving by starting to walk more rather than driving everywhere." My intention statement would then be something like this: "I'm now walking at least 15 minutes each day and with every step, I am becoming a healthier person. This is working out great!" I may not have totally believed it was going to work, but it was better than doing nothing and I tried to state my intention in a clear and positive way. Now it's your turn.

Goal 1 & My Intention –

Goal 2 & My Intention –

Goal 3 & My Intention -

PILLAR 2

Removing Obstacles

PILLAR 2

Removing Obstacles

I realize the fear of deep water is quite a common one. It may not be up there with the fear of public speaking, but I believe it is pretty close. To say that I had a fear of deep water would be a drastic understatement. For most of my life, I couldn't even walk beside deep water without getting a crushing feeling in my chest. While growing up in Newfoundland on the Atlantic Ocean, it was drilled into my head that open water was *bad and dangerous.* Although my parents meant well, they themselves both had a pretty strong fear of deep water so it was natural they tried to protect me with dire warnings.

As it turns out, my father didn't always have this fear. As a teenager, he and his friends would often walk down to a wharf and jump into the cold water to swim out to Gull Island. They didn't wear life jackets back then. But then on one tragic day they lost a friend in Gull Island Pond. They were all swimming along fine, when suddenly their friend got into danger. Despite their best attempts to save him, he was gone. I can't begin to imagine how terrible that must have felt.

I am not sure where my mother's fear of water came from but as long as I can remember Mom literally hated going anywhere near the water. I mean, we could not even drive down to the wharf if Mom was in the car. So as a result, I never wanted to go near water that was over my head and I developed a deep seated fear of open water.

Even with this fear at times I would try to push my own limits. One time in particular it could have been *game over*.

I was on Northern Bay Sands in Newfoundland with a group of my friends. We were all heading across the point that took us from the *little* sands to *big* sands.

However, that time of day, the water was at high tide and this day it was really windy too and the sign warned us not to attempt crossing due to a very strong undertow. My sensible friends turned around to walk up the rocky path in bare feet and take the long way around, but for some unknown reason I stayed staring at the waves. I remember thinking in my head: *I bet I can make it across and race them to the other side.*

Before I could think twice, I plunged into the water and was on my way to the nice sandy beach on the other side. *Then, whack!* A large wave hit me and pulled me under. Gasping for breath, I managed to get to my feet and edge my way closer to safety until I was hit by another wave. Then another and another, each time falling and fighting to get back to the shore. I still remember finally scrambling my way to safety and looking back at the ocean completely out of breath thinking *that was a really stupid thing to do*. It confirmed my original fear of water, and I never had any desire to go near deep water for many years!

But fast forward to my time up north in Iqaluit, and one day when I was running with Paul, I told him that I'd like to try a sprint triathlon. I admitted that I was a very weak swimmer and was terrified of deep open water, I wondered out loud how I could ever begin to develop the required swimming skills.

Paul had such a great idea that I couldn't say no. He said his son Christopher used to be a lifeguard and he was a really strong swimmer. Maybe he might be interested in teaching me to swim? Fortunately for me, Christopher was indeed keen about it, and we started to train every Tuesday and Thursday morning at 6:30 a.m.

This was in the Arctic, and many mornings I would wipe the sleep from my eyes, go outside into minus 30 to 50 degree C temperatures, clean off my van windows, and then pickup Christopher and Paul for our swim sessions. Paul laughed several mornings that instead of the Jamaican Bobsled Team, we were the Baffin Island Swim Team.

With these two for encouragement, I was able to get in the water and start practicing. It took some deep breaths, but I plunged in and bit the bullet. After the first few swimming sessions, I signed up for my first triathlon which was only nine months away. It was a lofty goal but with the support of my friends and family, along with Paul and Christopher's assistance and commitment to helping me, I kept moving forward.

You'd think that with all that training in the pool, I would have been a natural when I hit the water on the day of the event. But no. The open water swim portion was still terrifying. As I stood still looking at that large body of open water, most of the competitors were either in the water or getting into the water. I on the other hand was freaking out inside and taking slight steps backward. Fear made a strong appearance and my first thought was, *Wow, that's a lot of water out there, you don't have to do this, maybe you should go home.*

I quickly realized that training in a small eighteen- meter pool up North was much less intimidating than this large and frigid body of water. But then I thought of all my training and of all the people who supported me. Then I remembered the commitment I had made to them and to myself. I wasn't about to throw away all that work, effort and encouragement so I plunged into the water.

By the way, did I mention it was cold? In fact, if it had been one degree colder, the swim portion of the event would have been canceled that day. I'll never forget how cold that water felt on my face. Eventually the gun went off and I let the faster and more experienced swimmers fight for the front of the pack. When the initial flurry subsided, I began to swim.

I faced many challenges during this swim: some in my head and some in the water. The water that day had much more movement than I was used to while training in the pool. Also, where were those helpful lines on the bottom that I had grown so accustomed too?

I was elated when I completed that sprint triathlon, my first one! It was July 2011. Obviously, I didn't win the event, but that wasn't my intention. I had overcome my fear of being in deep water and that was such a natural high, I can barely describe the emotions I felt. I wasn't the fastest swimmer nor was I the slowest — but there's a high probability that I was the *proudest* swimmer who came out of the water that day. In my heart, mind, body and soul, I had already won.

I felt so alive having faced my fear in that situation where it was literally sink or swim. I have since learned that, more often than not, the obstacles we face are much bigger in our head then what we actually have to face in real life. And that was a lesson I have never forgotten.

What is Holding You Back?

So now we are digging into Pillar 2 which is about identifying what's currently holding you back and my goal is to help you to find a way around it. Your obstacles may be bigger or smaller than my example above, but everyone inevitably faces obstacles in life. Some are small, while others may be freaking huge, but over time, I believe that we each have the power to eventually move beyond them.

A good place to start in this discussion is to realize that the obstacles and barriers we face are most often rooted in fear. Those fears most often originate from limiting beliefs from our earlier years, or from belief systems that were, at some point, programmed into our subconscious mind. When the old beliefs that we programmed no longer serve us, our best action is to identify them, accept them and remove them so we can move on with our lives.

In addition to various fears, you may notice that you have other kinds of obstacles that are based on negative emotions such as anger, guilt and regret. Again, these kinds of barriers keep us from achieving our best life, and it is my belief that when we overcome or remove these negative barriers, we can finally live a life of passion, energy and joy. Whenever we conquer a struggle, we grow personally and develop a greater capacity to care for ourselves and to serve others.

The great news here is that the obstacles we face are actually *opportunities* to grow. This might seem like an odd concept to you, but stick with me for a bit and I will try to explain. If you can think of something that's been holding you back, try asking yourself: "What am I supposed to learn from this particular barrier, struggle or fear?"

In order to discover what is holding you back, you usually need to look inside yourself. One of the best ways I know to do this is the practice of daily meditation. It can yield amazing results which not only illuminate your fears, but allow you to begin to focus on more positive things and solutions to your fears, obstacles and barriers. In other words, meditation helps you overcome your past and create what you want to have in your life right now.

I encourage you to build a habit of daily meditation. The positive bi-products of these self-development practices will help you as you build on what you've learned so far, and as you move to the next section on identifying and managing fears, and discovering answers to your blocks and barriers by tapping into your own internal wisdom. You'll find some further instruction about meditation in the *Doyle* It In exercises at the end of this chapter. But first, let me talk about how to deal with fears that can arise as you go through life.

Managing Your Fears

Fear is inevitable but when managed effectively, it can help you achieve your goals even faster. As mentioned above, it's normal to have fears and from time to time, no matter how well you manage them, fears will surface and once again have to be dealt with.

I believe the most effective thing you can do when you feel fear about making a decision or moving ahead with your life is to *take action*. By taking action with regard to something that perhaps you haven't experienced before, you can change the initial feeling of fear into the excitement of doing something new. Once you face it, you can then also enjoy a sense of pride for having faced and overcome that fear.

You may have perhaps heard the saying: "Fear is a sign that you are about to do something amazing." To a certain degree, I believe in this statement, provided that what you wish to try is not truly dangerous. Obviously, we should maintain a certain level of common sense and caution in our daily activities. But in general, most activities that tend to cause fear, such as speaking in public, learning to swim, making an appointment to talk to our boss about something important, or breaking up with someone for example — these things are not directly hazardous to our health, and yet many people experience high levels of anxiety or fear about doing them.

In my case, my fear of deep water and not really knowing how to swim did not stop me from training and completing two triathlons. Although I *felt* the fear, I took actions in a certain order that made sense and I was eventually able to conquer my fear. By making a commitment to sign up for the race, and then believing in myself and working toward my goal each day, it was more than manageable to move past that initial enormous fear of deep water.

But of course, I do want to point out that I didn't do this alone, and this is an important lesson too. I had the full support of my family, friends and trainers who kept me accountable. I would highly recommend reaching out to other people in cases like this. When you have something you fear or an obstacle or barrier, try to find some supportive people to help you as you move through it. Never underestimate the power of a good network to support you when you face very difficult challenges. And once you overcome your own barriers, you can be the one to offer help and support to the next person who might be facing that or a similar situation.

If you remain stuck or paralyzed by fear, you don't get to fully enjoy your life. That's why I am a big proponent of identifying your obstacles and working through them. It is a continual process, whereby we have to embrace and overcome fear in life on a regular basis if we want to grow and feel alive inside.

You may wonder if you have within you the *capacity* to overcome your challenges, but I believe you do, because everyone does. Ordinary people and even the most successful people can all find ways to overcome the crap that might face them. And just to be clear, we don't magically just remove fear from our lives. What we do is learn to manage fear and although it's still present, we commit to taking action anyway because we are following our true power and purpose.

I am excited to say that I am at a point in my life as I write this section, that I have "taken the bull by the horns," and I am fulfilling my dreams and living my purpose. Instead of letting fear become an obstacle, I live by the belief that we should let our fears become the motivational jet fuel that propels us at lightning speed toward our goals.

True Forgiveness Will Set You Free

Another obstacle that can hold us back is anger at other people. Holding onto anger and holding a grudge tend to keep us bound up in our own chaos. I believe at some point on our personal journey, all of us will have to find forgiveness in our hearts and our minds for things and people that are holding us back. And I'm talking about both forgiveness of others and also forgiveness of ourselves. Holding on to anger will only harm you and not the person you are angry at. I always remember a quote by Buddha that says: "Holding on to anger is like drinking poison and expecting the other person to die." This is so true.

But you can release that anger and be free. You are the one in control of yourself. You can experience great freedom of your inner power when you practice true forgiveness. When we truly forgive, heal, and set new boundaries, over time we become grateful for all experiences. This is when you take back your personal power.

I do know first-hand that forgiveness will release anger and this is a good thing to do if you truly want to overcome what's holding you back and prepare to move forward in your life. In the introduction, I mentioned that my sister Darlene and her friend Karen were hit and killed by a drunk driver. It took many years but I eventually fully forgave the driver. A part of me actually wanted to meet him and forgive him in person. This may sound odd or even wrong to some people, but I believe that at our very core, at our soul level, all human beings are innocent and deserve forgiveness.

I actually had a very powerful dream where I met the driver in that accident and told him I forgave him. He wept deeply and thanked me and I felt a wave of emotion and was filled with feelings of pure love. It may have taken me a while to get there, to that point, but I have no regrets in life. Forgiveness is truly a freeing experience.

Remember, no one is perfect. I know I haven't always said and done "all the right things" in my life either, but this is the only life I have and it has taken me to the place where I am right now. I am at peace with myself and I have forgiven myself for the times I let myself down and when I let other people down. I have made amends when I could and I feel so much stronger and more at peace as compared to my earlier years when I found myself mired down with self-loathing, depressive thoughts, and anger toward others.

I know now that the more we practice being present and when we choose to only carry forward the positive memories and lessons from our past (not the anger), then we can experience a much greater level of vibrational expansion. Instead of spending so much of our lives looking outside of ourselves for answers, it's better to look inward because that is the only place we can find true happiness, peace and abundance.

What this means is that we all have a higher purpose and I feel that in order to fully harness our inner energy resources, we need to be at peace with others and with ourselves. I find myself lately appreciating the simple things in life and seeing beauty in places and things I never took time to see before.

Now let me close off this chapter with one more part of my story about overcoming my fear of deep water that brings my original story in this chapter full circle. After that, we'll move into the exercises and it will once again be your turn to Doyle It In.

Experiencing the Ripple
Effects of Releasing Fear

What happens when you overcome a big fear and your world really starts to open up? At the time, you may not know what that ripple effect will look like and how it will continue to expand your life in many other ways. But I assure you it will. Let me tell you about what happened to me, where I got to experience an incredible once-in-a-lifetime experience, all because I took the original steps needed to overcome my biggest fear.

This next part of my story picks up a few years after I swam in the triathlons and happened when friends of the family were visiting our place in Salmon Cove, Newfoundland. Andrew and Ingrid Peacock are an interesting, kind and inspiring couple and I consider them to be "salt of the earth." Andrew actually released his first book called *Creatures of the Rock* about three years ago and it was so awesome and inspiring to see him go through that process.

This particular night we were sitting around the living room drinking tea, having a yarn and playing music. During one of our conversations, Andrew asked me about kayaking because he noticed I had one on my front deck and he loved kayaking. I was quick to let him know I wasn't very experienced and that I would only take the kayak for a paddle around some of the neighbouring ponds on occasion.

When Andrew and Ingrid headed home that night, I stood on my front deck and called out just before he got into his car, "Give me a call sometime when you are going kayaking." Little did I know he would call from freshwater at 8:20 a.m. the very next morning with a cheerful invitation: "Hey, Ingrid thinks today is the day to paddle to the iceberg since there is no wind this morning." I told him, "Sure, see you in 20 minutes."

The second I hung up the phone, I thought: *What have I done?* I am not experienced and this isn't a pond we are talking about here. I was scared and excited at the same time when Andrew helped launch me in his extra sea kayak into the bay. I remember that nervous feeling as the boat started to float out and thinking, "Okay, Andrew, hurry up and launch your boat as well." We paddled approximately 45 minutes straight out into the bay with an eye on reaching a huge iceberg. At one point Andrew said, "Is it just me or are we not getting any closer?"

I knew that depth perception when you're out on the water can sometimes be a little off but eventually we did get closer and we could hear the distinct sounds of the iceberg, up close and personal. The waves and currents make all kinds of holes and waterfall-like sections in icebergs and this creates a high volume affect of rushing water. It was scary but at the same time so exhilarating and exciting!

It's hard to explain the soaring emotions of fear and exhilaration as they ran through me during our outing which lasted almost two hours out on the water. My experience and personal growth from doing that morning paddle with Andrew is hard to even measure. I felt so alive and extremely proud of myself for moving so far out of my comfort zone: from a swimming pool in Iqaluit, to the open swim of the triathlons, now to communing with an iceberg in its natural habitat. Listening to it sing to us. *Incredible.*

Andrew took several photos that day on our outing and for some reason one particular picture spoke to me in volumes. It was of me in the kayak and the look on my face was extraordinary joy and peace that I felt in that moment. Since then many other people have commented on this photo too. They are inspired by it and I love that this simple photograph can offer them a vision of what they can achieve when they face their own biggest fears.

I truly wish for you to experience the freedom and joy of living fully, confidently overcoming your fears and obstacles as they arise. So now, with that picture in your mind, it's time for you to *Doyle It In* and practice these techniques for yourself.

Doyle It In Exercise #4:

Tap Into Your Inner Energy and Wisdom

Meditation is an effective way to help you stay connected to your source and live in the present moment. Another tremendous activity to try is yoga which can help you develop a stronger mind, body and spirit connection that increases once you get into a regular yoga practice.

Within meditation and yoga you get to experience a quiet mind, which allows you to tap into your internal wisdom which has so many answers to your questions in your life. In the quietness, certain ideas and insights will come to you, giving you guidance toward forgiveness, clarity, and how to overcome the barriers that are holding you back.

You'll quite likely also notice that when you meditate or practice yoga, it helps ideas and energies flow more freely within you. When you are quiet, the positive energy fills you up and the beneficial boost of energy continues even after the session, as you continue with your day.

Some people think meditation means having to sit for an hour in total isolation in an effort to find your "inner chi." But like most of the lessons in this book, meditation is also an activity that you can start anywhere, by just taking small steps, and you can still get huge benefits over time.

Getting started on meditating can be as simple as making time to sit still, focus on your breathing, and try to slow your mind. You may only do it for two minutes your first few times and from there, you can slowly increase it to longer periods of time as you develop your meditation practice into a regular habit.

Other people find that starting with a guided meditation works for them. That is when you listen to a gentle voice walking you through breathing exercises and taking you on sort of a daydream to refresh your mind. You can find many different kinds of online meditation practices for free on the web and I would encourage you to find a practice that works for you and get started, one step at a time.

The benefits of yoga are similar but also extend to relaxation of both your physical body and your mind. As mentioned above, yoga really lets your internal energies flow through you while you release negative emotions and thoughts, and you let in positive light. Because there are so many elements of meditation within yoga, you may well find it an amazing way to create great clarity in your life and tap into the answers within yourself.

I love taking time to disconnect from my busy day to reconnect to my higher self. And you can too. We all have amazing energy and inner power that can be harnessed through meditating on a regular basis.

Doyle It In Exercise #5:

Get to Know Your Obstacles and Fears

Once you are feeling calm and focused, this next exercise will help you work on removing obstacles and managing fear. So before I ask you to list your possible negative emotions, beliefs, obstacles, and fears, I've included a few questions below. These questions are designed to help you do a little digging and hopefully begin to identify some of the main barriers that have been holding you back. Yes, it's time to dig in again. Take a deep breath and just answer as truthfully as you can.

- Is there anyone you need to forgive in your life? Here's a hint: often "yourself" is a great place to start. Personally, I found that I was the main block in my own life for many years.
- Do you have any regrets in life?
- If you answered yes, go home. No, just kidding of course. Almost all of us have had regrets. So if you answered yes, then write down what regrets you currently have.
- Are you holding on to anger? Why and against whom?
- Does fear often stop you from doing the things you'd like to do in life? What does this feel like?
- Do you often worry about your finances?
- Are you often stressed over things and situations that you have zero control over?
- Is your health and lifestyle in check? Think about your sleep patterns, nutrition, fitness levels and so on.

Once you have answered the questions above, you are ready to proceed to this next part of the exercise. Based on the three goals that you set in Doyle It In Exercise #3 from Chapter I, what do you feel are your current obstacles? For now, just list 1-3 obstacles that are most relevant.

Obstacle 1 -

Obstacle 2 -

Obstacle 3 -

Now ask yourself the following questions, with these obstacles in mind:

- What do I have to gain by overcoming these particular fears, obstacles, or barriers?
- What is the cost of holding on to these fears, obstacles, or beliefs?
- What needs to change to move past these limiting patterns?
- Am I ready and willing to make the changes required to move past these current blocks?

On a scale of 1 to 10, how important is it for you to get past these obstacles? Rank each of the 3 obstacles listed above on this scale from 1 to 10, with 1 being not very important to 10 being absolutely essential to overcome. This last part of the exercise will help you decide which obstacles are the most important ones to start focusing on.

Obstacle 1 -

Not very Important   Absolutely essential

1 2 3 4 5 6 7 8 9 10

Obstacle 2 -

Not very Important   Absolutely essential

1 2 3 4 5 6 7 8 9 10

Obstacle 3 -

Not very Important   Absolutely essential

1 2 3 4 5 6 7 8 9 10

Doyle It In Exercise #6:

Overcome Your Obstacles and Fears

When it comes to overcoming fears, barriers and obstacles, I believe that we all have *personal power* to do so but sometimes we are afraid to really harness it. I strongly encourage you to try, and again, you should consider seeking outside resources or experts to help you if you truly need some further support or encouragement.

Really my best advice is to look at the most essential things you need to overcome and determine some initial smaller steps you can begin with that you feel that *you can do*. Even if that is just to do some research into the problem or seek out what resources are out there for you, those are good first steps. Speaking to someone such as a coach, counselor or close friend can also be very powerful because just by saying it out loud, you have then set the intention that you wish to overcome a specific obstacle or fear. As you take one small step at a time, be kind to yourself and continue to stay grounded.

In addition, I have found that taking personal development courses has been very effective in helping me open up my internal energy flow and really tap into my inner strengths. I tend to recommend many good resources to my clients on a customized basis, since a number of my clients are just at the start of their journey to tap into their own inner power.

In particular, many seekers find that the lessons within *A Course in Miracles*, which is published by The Foundation for Inner Peace, are a good place to start if you wish to open up your mind to these powerful and proven universal spiritual principles. Many other current bestselling self-help authors and experts today have drawn on these same universal spiritual lessons, so you should be able to find a number of related resources depending on the style of material that speaks to you.

Between the courses I took, the books I read, and the experts I worked with, I felt I got a solid grounding and developed a repertoire of many useful techniques that served as the beginning for me in my own healing, forgiveness process, and the energy shifting that needed to happen to loosen up some of the long-held beliefs. These were stuck deep in my subconscious mind and I no longer needed them in my life.

You may also find that energy work such a Reiki balancing may be useful to loosen up long-stuck emotions that you are now ready to release.

I know this may sound strange if you are not familiar with energy work and energy shifting but I can say first-hand that it is very powerful. I recall once when I was doing an emotional clearing process on myself in a workshop one day, with a facilitator helping me, I found myself at a part in the process where I was instructed to say out loud, *"I am innocent."* I couldn't do it. I didn't realize how much guilt that related to my past that I had kept buried deep inside until that day.

I tried to voice the words, "I am innocent," but instead my whole body shook in waves of emotion as it flowed through me. But after crying uncontrollably for a while, I was finally able to say: "I am innocent." Just saying those words was such a freeing and uplifting moment in my life. I suddenly felt clearer, lighter and happier.

If you are feeling that you would like to clear buried emotions from your past, I encourage you to find a reputable energy practitioner in your area who assists with this kind of personal transformation work. Or you might also check out Sandy Levey's website. She is a person whom I worked with and whom I can personally recommend. www.sandylevey.com

PILLAR
3

Developing a
Positive Mindset

PILLAR 3
Develop a Positive Mindset

Although I didn't start drinking until my last year of high school, I quickly made up for lost time and was almost instantly known as the life of the party. I guess it was a combination of my chugging ability, my fun entertaining nature, and my talent to sing and play guitar. As a young adult, it was mostly harmless and fun, but as the years went by I could see the drinking and lost nights were getting out of control.

When I drank, I usually would just get funnier and laugh louder, but on occasion I would become overly jealous and this put stress on my relationships. My struggle with alcohol went on for almost two decades. It wasn't uncommon for me to drink 20 or 30 double rum and cokes in a night. I remember drinking for 15 hours and then going on to play a show and then I continued to drink until the wee hours of the morning. I loved going on long binges for days. When I was employed full-time, I had to be sober at least from Monday to Friday, but every weekend was wide open for uninterrupted boozing.

Straight out of high school, I started playing in a band and touring around Newfoundland. I had so many great experiences but this lifestyle definitely affected my health especially as I got older. Fast forward several years later and I was then living and working in Iqaluit, Nunavut.

My very good friend still today, Andrew Molloy and I started a band called The Northern Ramblers. We eventually were roommates at 301 White Row in Iqaluit and life got pretty wild. I can tell you that stories about those "301 White Row Days" are like legend because our place was known as *party central*. If those walls could talk, there'd be a lot of great stories. Unfortunately for me there would also be stories of struggle, severe hangovers, depression, feeling isolated, and being out of control. It was extremely hard for me to remain my positive upbeat self because I just hated the person I was when I drank to excess and I would be out of control.

As I mentioned in Chapter 1, once my binge drinking started to affect my relationships, my work and my health, I knew I would have to find a way to shake myself out of it. But at the time, my mindset was so poor and clouded that I couldn't see the forest for the trees. I even hit what I *thought* was rock bottom, and that didn't seem to be able to get me off that destructive track.

I wasn't sure at first if I would be brave enough to share this next part of my story with you, but I've decided to include it because I want you to understand just how much of a mess I was in. One night in 2008, after yet another night of way too much drinking, I woke up in the local jail. I wasn't causing any trouble but I had literally passed out on my walk home, only four steps from my apartment stairs. The RCMP officers had apparently asked where I lived but I was so drunk that I couldn't answer them, so for my safety they put me in the drunk tank overnight.

It was a horrible feeling to wake up and not know where I was. I felt so lost, tired and scared. I was seriously hung over and had a sore neck from sleeping on the small metal bed. I remember looking around the room and I saw that there was another person in there as well. He looked pretty hung over but seemed relaxed and not very concerned considering where we were.

When he saw that I was awake, he said hi and I said hi back. "Is this your first time in here?" he asked and I nodded, yes.

"Not my first time," he said with a slight grin as if it was no big deal. At that point I was still trying to piece together the night before and slowly getting my bearings.

All I could think was that I must have blacked out at some point. I was very lucky it was not wintertime because it could have been down to minus 50 degrees C outside. Sadly, it has happened that if you pass out in the cold on such a night in a northern community, you could die. Given the state I was in, that officer could have ended up calling the morgue. This terrible thought came back to me many times after that experience, but believe it or not, it was still not enough to make me quit drinking.

The actual urgency to make the change was triggered by two things that happened that Spring. First, I found myself at over 200 pounds for the first time in my life and I was becoming depressed an unhealthy. Just to put this into perspective, I am naturally a smaller type build and I weighed a whopping 115 pounds in Grade Twelve. But even more important to me was the light of my life,

I told you about him in Chapter 1, my son Timothy. He means the world to me.

I had been told many times by the doctors that I would not have children due to a very low sperm count. I remember talking to Molly one day about this and she was pretty sad and feeling down about the idea of never having children. I clearly remember saying to her that if it was meant to be and when the time was right, we would have a child together. I fully believed this with all my heart and in less than a year, Molly was indeed pregnant.

Timothy became my inspiration the moment he was born; that night was the most precious and amazing experience I have ever had. He was truly a miracle of life that instantly warmed my heart. That's why I almost felt like I was drowning in guilt when I realized that I was too hung over to play with him. Since he was then a toddler and growing up so quickly, I feared he would soon be old enough to notice my drinking and negative habits. I mean, *What kind of a role model could I be with my life spinning out of control?*

I needed a big shift in my life and I did it. I was determined to replace the feelings of guilt and fear with a more positive frame of mind, otherwise I would never rise above it. Fortunately, once I made this decision to kick the drinking and get my life back on track, another personality trait of mine came roaring to the forefront.

I've never been a person to do anything half-way. No matter what I take on, it's always been all or nothing. So sure enough, when I gave up the heavy drinking, I rather quickly replaced it with a pretty regimented fitness program. I didn't really realize this was happening at the time but eventually it became clear to me that exercise had become my outlet to cope with all the changes around stopping drinking and giving up my hard-living lifestyle.

Along with this, I sought out ways to improve my general outlook on life, moving it out from under all those feelings of depression and hopelessness. I tried to be thankful each day for what I did have, especially that my family had stood by me during the dark days and they were still there. I was thankful for my work and that I could still entertain a crowd. It was odd at first to be on stage stone-cold sober but I could still do it.

Soon I was being asked more and more often to entertain at fundraising events for people and causes that were close to my heart. When I gave to others, I got far more back in self-esteem and warm feelings than I ever gave out. Those experiences were magical and really elevated my whole mindset.

I was amazed how well these new techniques really worked. Within a few months, I was able to replace my destructive patterns of behaviour and my depressed mindset with a brighter and more hopeful outlook on life. It wasn't easy some days but I worked hard every day to continue on the more positive path.

When I look back on this period, I am kind of surprised that taking my body weight from 204 pounds down to 140 wasn't the most drastic change I experienced. What was even more dramatic was that once I infused my life with a more positive, grateful and giving mindset, I discovered that I had so much more energy, more confidence and I felt more powerful and alive than I could ever remember feeling before in my life.

And it occurred to me that if I could do this and feel so much better, I could become a beacon to teach others these same principles. Thus I became an entrepreneur, the Five Pillars were born, and I've been sharing this message ever since.

Why Work on This Mindset Stuff?

When I'm leading a group or teaching a course, what I hear very often is people will say that they already consider themselves to be a "positive person." And sometimes when we start talking about this part of the content, I can hear them thinking, "Oh boy, here we go again with this *positive mindset* stuff." And when asked, some of them say: "I am not a pessimist. I just like being realistic." Regardless of where you're at right now, I truly believe that when you consciously work on developing a positive mindset, you can and will add value to your life.

There is always something new to learn, or to be reminded of, that can keep you expanding the current vibration in this area of your life. I believe that a positive mindset is indeed a choice and it's a habit that can be fine-tuned over time. Every person can benefit from an elevated mindset and this chapter shares some practical ways to get there.

In fact, keeping a positive mindset is the single most powerful and important factor in achieving the kind of life you really want, one where you live fully every day. Successful and happy people strive to remain positive and they remain open to the unlimited possibilities their life offers them. Whenever I speak on this topic, many quotes by Jim Rohn come to my mind. Jim was a leader, speaker, motivator and author whom I like to learn from and he summed up this topic this way: "Success is something you attract, by the person you become."

What these Pillars are helping you to do is become the type of person who attracts good things. This happens when you live in more alignment with your core beliefs, because this state gives you *inner synergy*. This means that on any given day, the majority of your thoughts and actions are on the same frequency as your core desires.

At first, *inner synergy* isn't very easy to understand or measure. Try thinking about it this way: when you are full of joy and happiness then you are connected to your source energy or in a state of *inner synergy*. One of the best ways to become truly aware of your inner self is to take time for yourself.

I've set this up in an exercise at the end of this chapter, but basically this is about scheduling quiet time three times a day to relax, reflect, process things in your mind, and just be. I really encourage you to try it. It might seem to someone else that you're *doing nothing* but that's not the case. What you are doing is taking time for yourself and this activity benefits everyone you interact with for the rest of the day. It helps you stay grounded, able to see the big picture, and remember what is truly important to you in your life.

When you take time to sit quietly, it puts your whole system back into a state of balance or *inner synergy*. When you have balance, your mind can function at its best and your foundation is solid. Sustainable positive changes are fully supported when you have an unwavering foundation. The next Pillar will address this concept of foundation more, but for now, just start to think about how all these concepts build on each other and interrelate.

When you do spend quiet time in contemplation, always focus on the things you want in life, rather than the things you don't want. When negative thoughts and negative self-talk come up in your mind, simply allow them to flow without judgement, and they will soon pass.

Speak Kindly to Yourself

This is a good time to bring up how important it is that you work to overcome negative self-talk. I believe that when you put yourself down, it can be a sign that you haven't fully forgiven yourself or that you are holding onto something from your past that you no longer need. I strongly advise that you watch your inner dialog, which is how you speak to yourself in your head, and work to ensure that your self-talk is mostly positive.

As you have probably heard before, we are our own worst critic. The next time you find yourself speaking in a negative tone to yourself or about yourself, just consider this question: *Would I talk to others the way I am currently talking to myself?* More often than not, the answer will be no. Developing the habit of positive self-talk will not only make you feel better inside, but it will also radiate outward and cause positive changes in your outer world. Positive self-talk is an absolutely key element in developing a positive mindset. And silencing your own inner critic is one of the most powerful things you can do for yourself. The good news is that the more you practice positive self-talk, the less noisy your inner critic will become. We are our own biggest obstacle and also our greatest asset. The one we mainly fuel, will be the one that thrives.

Follow the Beat of Your Own Drum

Do you sometimes find yourself worrying about what other people think about you? Most people do have a tendency to worry about this but they shouldn't. This concept used to bother me because I thought people were always judging me and I had to be my "best behaviour" at all times. *But why?* Why should I care?

Here's an example of how I experienced this worry recently and what I did about it. A few weeks ago, I was in my back garden doing a workout using kettle bells, which are large cast-iron ball-shaped weights with a single handle. I had one in each hand and as the sun was shining, I thought to myself how much I'd like to be by the river as I did my workout. At first I thought, no, I can't walk down my street and follow the walking trails to the river side with kettle bells in my hands because what would other people think or say? They'd think I was crazy.

But then, fortunately, I allowed myself to really think about this and a new thought process presented itself. It seemed silly to worry about what others might think and what was the big deal anyway? So I took both kettle bells and headed for the river trails near my home. I enjoyed the fresh air, the sounds of the flowing river, and the feeling of being outside my usual comfort zone. People did indeed walk by me on the trail but they either went on about their business unaffected by my routine or I got a smile and even heard a few encouraging words.

Then three days ago, I was out on my usual brisk walk and headed to do my stair sprints close to the railroad bridge near my home. As I approached the stairs, I saw that, lo and behold, a man was doing kettle bell swings and then proceeding to do stair sprints. I made sure to time it so I wasn't in his way as I did my stair sprints, but at one point I could see that both of us worked out even a little harder because we had company that day. Strangers, no words spoken to each other but none were needed. We had the same goal. We shared the same space. No one cared what we looked like or what we were doing and we both had a great work out.

I smiled to myself and realized this was yet another lesson for the day. When you are being true to yourself as you proceed through your day, you very often motivate other people to do the same. My advice is not to be afraid to follow your own intuition because it will naturally bring you into personal alignment *(or inner synergy)* and that is where powerful creation begins. Don't worry about what other people are thinking. Just do what feels right for you.

Harnessing the Power of Gratitude

As you begin to give yourself permission to think more positively and develop your own healthier mindset, and as you strive each day to be in alignment with yourself, it is important to add a good dose of gratitude to your daily routine. Without doubt, being thankful is one of the most powerful techniques that I've discovered for shifting mindset. You know from my story above that gratitude helped me through my transition to a life without alcohol, but that was just the tip of the gratitude iceberg.

Today I make gratitude a daily habit. Each day I write down three things that I am grateful for. I can say with certainty that this practice works and it's such an easy first step to get you out of your own head and replace the negative thought patterns that might be holding you back from fully living your life. When you develop an attitude of gratitude, you'll find that you gain an increased appreciation for life in general and you'll begin see the good in others more often.

I find that the best time to practice gratitude is within your first hour of waking up. Write down three things you are grateful for and you'll be amazed at how this can set a positive tone for your day. You can be thankful for anything you have, think or feel in your life that you truly appreciate. Here are some items that are often on my gratitude list. I am thankful for my daily breath, a good night's rest, the sunshine, the trees, my family, my home, my health, my ability to learn, fresh water to drink and for good food on the table. Just last week, I wrote down that I was grateful for the obstacles I learn from.

And like so many of the practices I'm talking about in this book, you'll soon feel the ripple effects of this one too. In this case, as you build a stronger sense of appreciation for what you have in life, you will find that more and more good things will come to you. This is because you are focusing on the things you *want*, rather than putting an emphasis on *what you don't want*.

Giving to Others and Sharing of Yourself

I also encourage clients to harness the power of giving if they want to shift their mindset from negative to positive. You don't have to wait until you're financially well off in order to be able to give. You are forever rich internally with love and compassion and that is something you can give to others at any time. When you practice giving on a regular basis, you naturally start to shift your mindset and become an ever better version of yourself than you were before.

The reason giving is so important is that you grow exponentially when you contribute toward something outside of yourself. I have found great peace and joy in giving to local thrift stores and food banks throughout my life. Or it may be just a smile or a kind word to a stranger who really needs to hear it. When you think about it, it costs you nothing to be kind and compassionate, but it makes a tremendous positive impact on others.

I fully believe it feels better to give than to receive. It's rewarding to feel you are a part of something bigger than yourself. It was awesome when I lived in Nunavut because I got to be involved in all kinds of benefits and fundraisers where I would perform music or run the sound equipment.

The first project I did of this nature was when I volunteered twice a week for six months at the City of Iqaluit Youth Center. I gave free guitar lessons to some of the young people, and I worked with Amy Elgersma who later became the Director of Recreation for the city. I learned a lot from her because she has an authentic desire to help young people to grow and learn, and to become healthy and successful.

After the six months of lessons were completed, I recorded the kids playing and we released a CD called The Sounds of Youth. Although I had performed on CDs before, this was the first time I engineered a whole album. The proceeds from this CD went back into the Youth Center.

A few years later I was approached about an idea to raise money for the Women's Shelter and we basically created an Iqaluit Women and Song CD with local female singers. I recorded nine tracks from five performers and we asked some other people to donate graphics for the CD to keep the costs as low as possible. Proceeds went to the Women's Shelter and I was very happy to contribute my talents to it. The ripple effect that came back to me from these experiences was that I learned all kinds of practical details about live recording and production, about Inuit music, and about project management. These are skills that I have gone on to use many times over in my life.

You never know when you might find a time and place to impact someone else through a thoughtful gift. I remember one chance I had that was so nice. It happened when I was taking a course in Bellingham, Washington. There was a woman there who had a daughter who really wanted to learn how to play fiddle. Her mother had said that one day when she could afford it, she would get her a fiddle so her daughter could learn the instrument.

When I returned to Newfoundland after my trip, I went into a local music store and purchased a fiddle and shipped it to her. I later received a letter with a warm thank you and it went on to say that her daughter was now taking fiddle lessons and loving it. This just shows that we are all part of something bigger than ourselves and when we help others get what they want in life, we ourselves become truly blessed.

Asking for Help and Learning to Receive

I was born to be of service and all my friends know that about me. I would help my friends to move, renovate, clean, and build. You name it I was there to help. This is a positive thing but at the time, I wasn't open to asking for help or receiving for myself.

But after much self-investment, inner work and growth, I now am open and I love receiving from others. I learned my first lesson on this topic from Sharla Mulley, a really good friend of mine. We were talking one day and she found out that I had moved apartments on the weekend. She asked me right away who helped me. When I said no one, I did it myself and it took a lot of trips, she got upset with me. "Michael, you are so dependable and always there to help everyone when they need something, why didn't you ask for help?" she wanted to know.

Then she went on to say that if I moved again, I better ask for help. Well I did indeed move again and that time I did ask for help. Sharla was one of the people I called and she was on my door step. That all happened about ten years ago but recently

I was visiting Sharla and I was reminded about how she helped me realize that I deserved to have others help me sometimes. It was a lesson I needed at the time and I am grateful she pushed me to learn to *ask for help*.

I love the fact that acts of kindness are happening all over the world at any given point in time. Sometimes you are on the giving end and sometimes you will receive. I think we all have the ability to give and receive and we all are able to see the *divine essence* in everyone. Love is an infinite energy source that we can all harness, share and never run out of. No matter how much love we give throughout our lives, we will leave our physical form someday with a never ending supply of love still within us. So feel free to share your love, compassion and talents with others. It will bring you a sense of fulfillment that only contributing to others can bring.

You may be aware of these techniques and you might do them occasionally, and that's good. But when you bring a greater awareness to them and build daily habits around them, that is when you will really be able to elevate your current mindset. I am fully confident that you'll see positive changes almost immediately and enjoy higher clarity and increased energy from just being more positive, thankful and giving. And remember, it's OK to *want* more in life, but appreciate what you have, while you work toward what you want. Now it's time to *Doyle It In* yourself and try the following exercises to build a more positive mindset.

Doyle It In Exercise #7:

Disconnect to Reconnect

To jumpstart yourself toward a more positive mindset, take time three times each day just for yourself. I find it best to do this when you wake up, again around mid-day, and at night. I call this process "disconnecting to reconnect" and you actually schedule this quiet time into your day with the intention to relax, reflect, process things in your mind, and just be. If you want to combine your quiet time with a meditation or mindfulness session, by all means do so. But just sitting quietly is also truly transformational.

There is a solid principle behind this exercise. In the same way that your physical body benefits from having a certain amount of recovery time after a workout, then you should make time for your mind and spirit to have sufficient recovery time from your busy daily activities and commitments.

To do this, turn off all your devices and sit quietly. Take some deep breaths and visualize your whole inner system gently returning to a state of balance or *inner synergy*. Feel yourself becoming centered and more grounded. Stay with this feeling for 5 or sometimes even 15-20 minutes. Afterward, I think you will notice that you'll be better able to see the bigger picture and you won't lose sight of what is truly important to you in your life as you resume the hustle and bustle of your busy day.

Personally I like to take quiet time for myself like this every morning and at least once during the day when I can sit by myself for about 10 minutes to recoup. Then each night, I make it a point to relax, let my mind process things, and just be in the moment one more time. Think about this technique as a way to recover from your outward stressors on a regular basis.

And it is worth repeating: when you spend quiet time in contemplation, always focus on the things you want in life, rather than the things you don't want. If negative thoughts and negative self-talk come up in your mind, see it happening without getting to involved, and change your thought patterns away from the negative.

Doyle It In Exercise #8:

Be Thankful Every Day

No matter where you are in your life, you can be certain that many other people out there would love to have what you currently have. Even if your life is not going the way you may want, try your best to be grateful and accept where you are. Acceptance of where you are right now is very important in order to move beyond your current situation or any daily worries. Here are some practical daily steps to help you develop a practice of gratitude.

- Find a nice journal that you can use for your daily gratitude entries and reflections.
- Each morning, within the first hour of waking up, write three things you are grateful for.
- Once you make this a practice, add an extra step and write down why you are grateful for these things.

Doyle It In Exercise #9:

Find Ways to Give to Others Daily

This exercise is to encourage you to give to others every day. Remember, you don't have to be rich to give to other people. A little goes a long way and sometimes just a lending hand, a listening ear, or a few kind words at the right time can be very powerful in helping others through a rough patch.

If you currently have a regular charity that you support or an organization that you sponsor, that's great. But still, try to remain open to additional ways that you can give back and serve others.

Start by making a list of the places you have recently donated to and examine why you chose to provide support to them. This may spark an idea or an even deeper way you can continue to make a difference.

Remember, you don't always have to provide financial support. There are many ways to give. For example, see if there is a local organization where you could volunteer once a week or once every two weeks. Even once a month is good.

Think about what you are good at and how those skills could be used to help someone in need.

Commit to helping someone in need whenever possible. We all have those moments when our heart tells us to help in some way, but sometimes fear and ego can cause us to lose confidence. Think about a time you drove by someone and thought to yourself afterward, "Oh, I should have stopped." Don't dwell on what you should have done; instead resolve to take action next time, even if it's something small like letting someone onto the road during traffic, opening doors for others, or letting someone behind you in line go before you at the grocery store if they seem to be overly stressed or upset that they are late.

PILLAR

4

Building a Solid Foundation

PILLAR 4

Building a Solid Foundation

You might never suspect if you saw me speaking on stage today, but for more than 30 years, I absolutely hated the idea of public speaking. Even though I performed with total enthusiasm as a musician, the minute you took away my guitar and gave me a different subject to talk about, I was completely out of my element, like a fish out of water.

This came to a head when I launched my coaching business back in 2016, because I knew that being able to speak to groups would be a key element of my overall business. I was not going to be successful if I kept freezing up or getting tongue-tied when anyone would hand me the microphone to speak.

When I looked at the bigger picture, I realized that I needed to put in place a *better foundation* for this new career path, and I wondered where in the world to start. I realized it wasn't just better skills in public speaking that I needed but a wide range other resources and knowledge. I thought it would be great to have a network of positive people to keep me accountable and motivated and I would need other professionals to lend skills in online marketing and so many other business development aspects that I didn't know much about at the time.

I started to get a bit overwhelmed at the prospect of setting up a whole new base, but it had to be done. Then of course there was that *fear* again, rearing its ugly head. But I knew now I could face these fears. I just had to make a list, break it down and take one small step at a time.

Sure enough, I found a course on public speaking and joined the Forest City Toastmasters here in London, Ontario for awhile. If you want to get good at something, you have to do a lot of it, so I committed to actually giving the speeches they recommended. The first one was really nerve wracking but with each one I tackled, I gained increased confidence. The feedback the other Toastmasters gave me was very practical and encouraging, which I totally appreciated.

The next step was preparing to speak to an even larger audience, and I decided I would soon share my personal story to a group of several hundred people at a MoMonday's event. When I first put my name in to speak and was given a date here in London, Ontario, I was freaked out but also very excited. I knew that with determination and consistent action, I could rock that stage. This was the next step in the foundation that I needed for my new career path, so I practiced and practiced, putting my all totally into it. I did indeed rock that stage and I have gone on since then to do many other public speeches and facilitation of meetings and workshops.

Just to be clear, I am not fully over my fear of public speaking. It's maybe good to still feel a rush of excitement just before stepping out on stage, but now I can manage the fear better because I have a stronger foundation of experience to support my efforts.

Since my move to London in August 2015, I have been fortunate to experience countless synchronicities. The amazing people showing up into my life and supporting me have created a solid foundation which has been such a blessing. I am grateful for the people who are now in my circle because they have allowed me to move forward with both my plan and my purpose.

This new group I engage with are my *circle of influence* and I credit them with helping to support, motivate, and elevate me to new levels. No man is an island and I would never want to be. It's just so much better to have people around me whom I can trust and whom I can lean on. Let me just mention a few categories of people who now are part of my solid foundation of resources and you can get the picture.

Even though I am a trainer, I still have a personal trainer to help me stay in shape. I am a coach but I have an NLP coach who keeps me sharply focused on my own life path. If you're not familiar with it, NLP is Neuro Linguistic Programming and it is a way to identify the thinking patterns that can get in the way of your progress. NLP offers practical ways to change your thinking which in turn changes your life. I also found an amazing meditation guru who creates custom guided meditations. And I go to a Registered Massage Therapist (RMT) when I need to.

Then the list continues on the business side of things, and includes a great graphic designer, helpers in website development, technology consultants, a professional videographer when I need her, and an experienced editor. I put this group together over time so that I would have the foundation needed to grow personally and professionally while effectively growing my business.

And just before I wrap up this discussion, there is another fabulous system that I implemented in my life that has yielded amazing results. I am talking about my *mastermind group.* This is basically a group of like-minded people who have similar goals or vision. We built a joint intention that keeps each member of our group accountable and helps us all stay focused on the visions we want to manifest for ourselves in our lives and in our businesses.

Building a Solid Foundation

I realize it may seem a little strange that *building a solid foundation* is the fourth Pillar and not the first one. Here's the thing. I don't think it makes sense for you to start building your foundation when you don't have the clarity and other general skills to really make the best of it. That's why I made sure to explain the importance of clarity and intention first, then take you through how to overcome fears and obstacles, and then how to develop a positive mindset. Only with those elements and skills in place does it make sense to then create your actual *foundation.*

The way I look at it, it would make no sense to create the foundation for an A-frame house, only to realize that once you have more clarity, you really wanted a log home. Obviously, it's much better to begin setting a strong foundation for your life once you know *what you truly want.* And logically, you need a strong foundation in order to determine your next strategic action steps, which is the reason that Pillar 5 is about taking action.

So now I'd like to talk about how all these key elements we've been talking about come together to form the solid foundation that you need for your life:

1. ***Set bigger and bolder goals.*** This is the point when you raise the bar and become very clear on your bigger and more encompassing goals. You've had some practice setting goals for smaller parts of our life, so now start to consider setting bigger and bolder goals.

2. ***Develop a strong circle of influence.*** You may have heard this before but it bears repeating: the type of person you ultimately become is based on the average traits of the handful of people with whom you spend the most time. So choose wisely.

3. ***Commit to continuous learning.*** Never underestimate the importance of self-investment. It will enhance your life in many areas.

4. ***Take time for self-care.*** This lesson reminds you to take time to rest, relax, play, mediate, and enjoy the journey of life. When you are balanced and have inner clarity, all aspects of your life will be better.

5. ***Ask for help.*** You don't have to do absolutely everything yourself. Learn to both give and receive since this will make your life so much more fulfilling and far more manageable.

6. ***Pay attention to your nutrition and fitness.*** Without your health, no amount of systems, courses, routines, or mindset changes will be of any value. My common sense suggestions and a general overview of nutrition and fitness are in the Valuable Resources sections # 1

and # 2 at the end of this book. If you haven't read them over, do that now because you really can't be of service to yourself or others unless you are healthy.

Creating New Habits

Nate Green, creator of the book *Scrawny to Brawny*, wrote, "Habits make us, and habits break us." This really resonated with me. While on my personal journey of growth and healing, I was breaking many bad habits, and developing newer healthier ones. I know you probably know this by now, but truly I believe that a gradual positive progression over time is the best approach for making lifestyle changes.

There are several opinions on how long it takes to create a new habit. I don't think there is one exactly correct length of time. For some people it might take 21 days while for others it could take up to 60 days of consistently doing something before it becomes a solid habit.

So rather than stress about how long it takes, focus on doing the thing as consistently as possible until it becomes a seamless part of your daily routine. And remember, no one is 100% consistent so don't beat yourself up if you fall back once in a while. If you go off the r ails, and you will, just dust yourself off and tac k le the new habit again. Move forward and try again.

Setting Bigger and Bolder Goals

I hope you realize now that you are capable of achieving all of your goals. A big part of this is believing that you can. That's why we started out in Pillar 1 with simpler goals to get you jumpstarted into the process and to let you know, yes, *you can do it*. I often tell my clients to never underestimate the power of believing for it plays a critical role in the likelihood of reaching your goals.

You may have read other books or taken courses on goal setting and I believe the many different opinions and systems on this topic do have valuable points to make. One of the most popular frameworks for creative goals is to keep them "SMART". A Smart goal is: Specific, Measurable, Attainable, Realistic, and Time-Bound. I honestly feel that there is a time and place where this type of goal setting holds a purpose but I feel we need to raise the bar. I believe we all must, at some point in our journey start setting goals that both excite us and scare us. Goals that makes us play a bigger game and help us grow by raising our ambition.

I personally also have another system of goal setting that ensures we are fueling the physical, non-physical and the meta-physical. Try setting a goal for your mind, a goal for your body and a goal for your spirit. When we are intentionally fueling our mind, body and spirit daily amazing things will start to happen within you and for you.

Regardless of the system of goal setting you choose, don't lose sight of the *"why"*. You know now from your work in Pillars 1 and 2 that it might take reaching down through several of your own layers and overcoming fears in order to get to a deeper level within yourself before you truly understand your own "why" but I encourage you to keep digging until you get there. Once your goals stem from a place of core desire within yourself, you can and will be far more driven to achieve them.

I was honored and grateful to be included with other amazing and proven leaders in the world of health and wellness in a magazine publication and it was an achievement I had been striving for.

About a year before this, I had set rather lofty goals to see myself published alongside other high profile global leaders who are authentic in their approaches to fitness and health. I then took steps daily to confirm my own profile, credibility and experience, using the same authenticity I saw in them, as one of the many steps I took toward this goal. I also did quite a bit of networking and personal development to earn a place alongside the kind of leaders I aspire to become more like.

The added benefit to me of trying new things and pursuing bigger and bolder goals is that I realized how much more alive and inspired it made me feel. The simple act of attending inspiring talks, seminars and workshops allowed me to connect with like-minded people and I found it extremely motivating. Self-investment has significantly built u p m y confidence, clarity, energy levels, passion and ultimately ignited my purpose.

Not all your learning has to be work related. You might find that wall climbing, zip lining, or white water rafting can also be exciting and fun and these activities will help you build your character. Doing something new is always a little scary because of the unknowns. Try asking yourself this question: *When was the last time you did something for the first time?*

Make Time for Self-care and Balance

Like so many people, I expect that you may have been programmed to do, do, do, and go, go, go, in an endless effort to meet the demands and expectations of others. Being on the go can be awesome and fulfilling, as long as you are open to receiving and giving to yourself and remaining in balance between work and life. In other words, when you are making big changes in your life, don't lose yourself in the process. I highly recommend taking time for self-care which is about taking time for yourself and doing things just for the pure joy of them.

Here's a cautionary tale to drive home this idea. While living in Iqaluit, I worked full-time as a financial analyst with the government and was sometimes busy with two of my own companies on the side. I was going most of the time and I was all about doing. Kurt Vonnegut said, "I am a human being, not a human doing." So just remember we are human *beings* and not human *doings*. I can identify with this thought because when I didn't take any time for myself, I felt completely out of balance and out of control until I forced myself to stop all the manic *doing* and focus more on the quiet *being*.

It worked so well for me that now my approach to life in general is all about balance. Whether it's fitness, nutrition, building habits, or developing self-care routines, a gradual approach is always best. Maybe you already meditate, practice yoga, or do deep breathing. If so that's great but also remember to take time just to be and also make time to enjoy your life and have fun. Getting adequate sleep and booking in sufficient down time in your schedule will ultimately allow you to have more clarity and energy for life. We are all driven by clarity.

Doyle It In Exercise #10:

Become Better at Self-care

Here are a few ways you can improve your level of self-care to ensure you have a strong foundation upon which to take action on your goals.

- Think about the five people you spend the most time with outside of your home. Do you feel you need to make adjustments in your circle of influence? If yes, why? If no, why not?

- Are you comfortable asking others for help? If no, what can you do to improve this situation and move outside your usual comfort zone?
- Have you taken time to look at people who have successfully done what it is you are looking to accomplish and learn from them? What inspires you about them and why? How can you find out more about what has made them so successful? Commit to request an interview with them if you can.
- Do you have your fitness and nutrition in order? Please take time and answer honestly because it is vitally important.
- Do you often take time for yourself? If yes, how often and for how long? If no, explain why not?
- What are three self-care activities that you can start with right away? Commit to take action on at least one of them tomorrow and phase in the other two naturally over time.

Doyle It In Exercise #11:

Create Your Own Circle of Influence

As you could tell from my story at the beginning of this chapter, I fully believe the right support network will not only increase your chances of reaching your goals but it will also speed up the process significantly.

When you set out to find the people to help you grow personally and professionally, make it a point to create all those connections as authentically as possible. Don't rush out and select the first person or the first networking group you discover. Instead strive to really connect with each person and think about how you can add value to your connection with them.

In other words, set up each new person in your circle of influence in such a way that you both are able to give and receive within the relationship. If you seek connections for the sole purpose of personal gain for yourself, then your connections will not be as strong or loyal. But when you are genuine, you will connect with other truly genuine people who want to bring out your best, the same way you want to do for them.

I cannot stress enough that who you surround yourself with determines who you become. As Jim Rohn said, "You are the average of the five people you spend the most time with." That's why I suggest that you consider forming a mastermind group for yourself of 4 to 6 people who are committed to elevate themselves and help you and each group member to reach even greater personal and professional heights.

The duration and frequency of your mastermind meetings or calls can vary but I personally find that meeting every two weeks for an hour is manageable and productive. You can meet online if you live in different parts of the country. But in addition to your regular online meetings, you may want to meet up in person on a quarterly basis for a day or even a weekend-long session in order to really tap into the collective wisdom and power of the mastermind group. This will go a long way to fostering exponential growth for all the members.

Doyle It In Exercise #12:

Build Your Own Solid Foundation and Set New Goals

I know we touched on goals within Pillar 1, but they were just initial goals to get you moving in a more purposeful trajectory at that point. Now that you understand more about the importance of goal setting, my next suggestion is to continue to raise your own goals and the expectations that other people around you have of you. This way, you will become more accountable and this tends to significantly increase your chances of following through with both your powerful commitments and purpose.

Now it's time for a few questions to help you with this Pillar.

Take a moment to think about the six foundational elements talked about in this chapter:

- *Set bigger and bolder goals.*
- *Develop a strong circle of influence.*
- *Commit to continuous learning.*
- *Take time for self-care.*
- *Ask for help.*
- *Pay attention to your nutrition and fitness.*

Which of these would be your top three? Why? What are you prepared to do to strengthen your foundation in these top three elements?

1.

2.

3.

Do you currently have some bigger and bolder goals that you now want to work toward? If yes, what are they? Why are they so important to you?

1.

2.

3.

Think deeper now about the "why" and try to match the "why" up with a core values or core desire that you hold. The closer the "why" matches up with your core desires, the more you will be driven to achieve these goals.

PILLAR
5

Taking Effective Action

PILLAR 5

Taking Effective Action

Taking effective action is what ultimately makes things happen in your life. I've always been a "doer" so this was, at first, the simplest Pillar for me to get my head around. I have a certain knack and drive for getting things done and completed, but I know not everyone finds that this comes naturally to them.

My personal story about this Pillar is about a time when I had to apply all my knowledge of each of the Pillars in order to accomplish one big hulking project, something new and exciting that took me out of my comfort zone for sure. Specifically, I had to become clear, move past numerous obstacles, stay positive, be open to asking and receiving support, and I had to take effective action. Lots and lots of action, on so many big and small details.

I must admit when I was first approached about providing the sound for a new multi-cultural arts festival in Iqaluit, fear instantly set in. A lot was riding on making the Alianait Arts Festival a truly successful and memorable event. My self-talk quickly went from being excited to scared, with that critic in my head ready to cut me down to size: *Who are you to take on such a large task? What experience do you have with festivals?*

Up to this point, all my previous experience with festivals just involved me standing on stage with a guitar doing what I was used to doing, performing music. Setting up and doing all the live sound, that was a much bigger animal. But here's the thing: if we wait in life until we feel fully ready for a challenge, there is a high probability we'll never take the leap.

So despite the surge of opposing thoughts and emotions, I somehow said yes to facilitating the sound. OK. Big project. Deep breath. I knew that this cause resonated with my core values because I loved music and sound — music has always been one of my biggest passions. I didn't mind the idea of working long hours on something so exciting, so at least I had that going for me. But the rest of the details were going to be a big challenge to pull together.

The Alianait Arts Festival was something new for the community, so I had to start the planning so I could ensure we'd have enough sound gear for such a big event. My first step was to work out what exact gear we needed and how many hands-on-deck I would need for the event itself.

As I compiled a list of the gear I required, I thought about each of the places I could approach to get these things. I knew I needed to clearly communicate what I needed from each of them and for most of the businesses, I thought about what service I could give them in return that would be of value to them, so I could appeal to them to donate what they could. I really just wanted to pay for what I couldn't get donated, and that way I could stay within budget.

Since I knew a lot of the community businesses personally, I felt pretty good reaching out and asking for help. I started to call each person and business I knew that could help provide the range of gear needed. Fortunately, there were quite a few people who were happy to donate to such an exciting new event.

I then reached out to friends whom I knew that had enough knowledge to be stagehands during the shows. I gave them the schedule and clearly outlined the roles and responsibilities. I explained that I didn't have a big budget but it was a lot of hours and I would pay them for the day. I wanted them to know that I respected them and trusted them. I even had "Doyle Entertainment" t-shirts made for a professional look and some extra advertising.

It took a lot of calls, a lot of steps, a lot of negotiating, contracts, paperwork, and all the trimmings that go with a live event. But the good thing was that the more action I took, the more confidence I felt inside. By the time it came to fire up the sound and lights for the main show, I was ready to rock it out of the park.

I can still hear all the great bands who played and feel the energy of the crowd. It was incredible the sense of accomplishment I felt. I had so many people tell me what a great job I was doing and how the sound was superb. The friends whom I hired said I was awesome to work for and they were really pleased with the pay as well. But I think the coolest thing was just knowing that I was a part of something much bigger than myself. I was helping to put many Nunavut artists on the stage, in the media, and on the map. I am truly grateful to Heather Daley for the opportunity to provide sound for the Alianait Arts Festival. This festival continues to flourish and this wouldn't be possible without Heather's passion, energy, and vision.

And as with each of the Pillars in this book and with my own stories of self-discovery, this one too had some unforeseen benefits to me. By putting myself out there, and really giving my all to this festival, I built up my network and strengthened my connections in the industry. As a result, I went on to work on a lot of other gigs in Nunavut because of the exposure I received doing sound for this first festival.

Each time I did an event like this, my confidence and my prosperity mindset kept improving. I made sure that I always went a step above what was expected because it feels great to over-deliver. I realized that people don't mind paying more if they are getting the desired results, so I was able to make live sound production and project management an even bigger and better part of my overall revenue streams over time.

Don't be Afraid to Fail Forward

You can see from my story that I drew on all the principles learned within the five Pillars here, but I cannot stress enough that the main thing that made this successful was the fact I took action. I tell clients all the time to just start somewhere and go for it. You can always learn as you go but you need to commit *to get started*.

I realize of course that there may be times when you might fall short of a goal or an aspect of a goal. The important thing is to do it and learn as you go. Successful people fail often and they refer to this as "failing forward". Each time they try something and it doesn't work, they can adjust their approach and try again in a new way, so they are still moving forward.

The path to a goal is seldom a straight line and there will inevitably be highs and lows. I am not saying that once I said yes to doing sound for this festival, everything easily fell into place. In fact, I struggled from time to time either with my mindset or a logistical detail until I could get my courage back up or a plan to push through it. But overall I managed to stay focused, to use the support I had, and work hard. It just goes to show that if you have a determined and strong work ethic and take consistent action, you will increase your chances of success every time.

So indeed, the take-home message for Pillar 5 is that the best ideas, plans, support systems, and positive mindsets will only yield results if you find a way to take effective action on a consistent basis. I learned this the hard way and I am now fully invested in taking effective action with any new things that I tackle.

Using Systems to Catapult Your Efforts Forward

I love systems because I find a system of doing something makes it so much easier. For example, I have taken courses on how to be productive and really leverage my time. It's amazing! And I believe that if you put your efforts into even just a portion of my personal take-away advice in this section, you will see incredible results.

Here's an example. As much as I love a good "get-to-do-list" and I know it can serve a purpose, I don't suggest that you start your day with this list. I actually would suggest that instead you start the day by setting an intention for your day before doing anything else. One of my favorite intentions is to ask that the majority of my time that day be spent on priority items which are directly linked to my goals. It is key to mention, my main intention for any day, is to ensure my energy, thoughts and actions serve the highest good of all involved.

In the *Doyle It In* exercises within this chapter, I list a number of techniques that you can use to plan and manage your days and weeks to ensure that effective action becomes the norm in your life. Yes, I know life happens but the key is to spend the majority of your time on track with your plan.

I am a big fan of Hal Elrod and his book *The Miracle Morning*, as well as his podcast series. This morning routine worked for me for several months and really helped create new "go-to" habits. He suggests that these 6 steps should be made up of 6 habits that are stacked or sequenced in a certain order. Then you just make the whole *stack of actions* a habit which you learn to repeat every morning, and this allows you to adopt a number of good habits all at one time. This system spoke to me and I found it really easy to adjust to because the sequence itself becomes a new habit.

I also recently added the practice of writing down my intentions for the day and it has really helped me to stay motivated, on track and productive. Your daily intentions are not quite the same as a "get-to-do-list". Yes I said "get" to do. This slight change automatically helps you have more gratitude for the daily task you perform. A list is helpful throughout your day but ensure to follow through on the daily intentions you set. Again every person is different and I encourage each person to try different methods or systems to see what works best for them.

Taking Control of Your Morning

This is the way I take control of my morning. First I take a minimum of an hour every day when I first wake up to focus on just me and my vision. Upon waking I make my bed, drink a glass of water, do breathwork, meditate and then take a cold shower. I follow this with either a short walk outside or some type of light movement. Sometimes I do *mirror* work before I start my breakfast routine, which is to repeat positive statements to myself while looking in a mirror.

If you are a heart centered entrepreneur like me, I expect you have passion, energy, vision, good intentions, and no shortage of ideas. However, we can easily get a little distracted with squirrel syndrome which is also sometimes called, "ooooh, another shiny object". If you are this way, then scheduling your week so working on priority tasks is paramount. This allows you to work on your business instead of just in your business.

When you choose new habits, try to make sure each habit is productive and effective, and that it will efficiently get you closer to your goals. Many people believe if they are busy and have a day where they check off lots of "get-to- do" items, then it was a productive day, but this is not always the case. You see depending on how the list was organized, or not organized, it may just have been a busy day of spinning your wheels and using up your energy. As I said, I get around this problem by clearly writing down my intention for the day first thing in the morning, and that keeps me focused on the priority tasks which are the ones that will eventually get me to my goals over time.

Setting daily intentions will make the difference between spending your day in reaction mode or in strategic action mode. Even though unexpected things can happen and you will rarely be able to stick 100% to your plan, if you do manage to do it 85% of the time, then that is far more efficient than being in reaction mode all the time.

Staying organized doesn't have to be a struggle. Take the time to develop the required habits to manage your day, week, month, year, and so on. Write down all the items you have going on and ensure you itemize and prioritize them.

How the Wise Ones Do It

As I wrap up this chapter and this book, I would just like to revisit the topic of how to effectively set and achieve your goals because it will further illustrate how successful people use the principles I have been presenting throughout the book.

In particular, I'd like to introduce you to several successful people in my circle of influence whom I am inspired by. Their full interviews are in the Valuable Resources sections #3, #4 and #5 and I do encourage you to read their longer profiles. But here are just a couple of highlights from them about goal setting.

The first person I asked to participate by submitting her success tips was Maureen (Mo) Hagan who is Chief Operating Officer for canfitpro at their head offices in London, Ontario. I admire her incredible leadership qualities and how she has always been a goal setter, even from her teenage years. Mo says that everything you do starts with belief, and that your beliefs shape your attitude, and your attitude shifts your thoughts. Thoughts shape your words and words lead to actions.

Her most important tips for goal setting are to begin with a success mindset where you visualize that you have already achieved your goal and then follow through with daily and disciplined action in pursuit of that goal. She says that each day it is very important to protect your beliefs, attitude and thoughts from those who may not support your dream. She also knows the value of verbalizing and visualizing your goal each morning and acting that day as if you have achieved it. Then each evening reflect on your progress.

The second highly successful person I asked to participate with a profile is my brother Patrick Doyle. Patrick is driven, successful, and I am inspired by his effective leadership. He worked his way up in the security industry and is the CEO & Founding Partner of Scarlet Security & Risk Group. (SSRG) Patrick is a master at building customer loyalty and creating hugely valuable strategic partnerships and local stakeholder engagement. As the CEO for the past fifteen years, his focus has been to expand the company's assets across the country using the successful model he pioneered in the North whereby they worked closely with First Nations and were able to set up mutually beneficial partnerships in order to supply security services to large industrial environments.

Pat says there are so many key elements that help people reach amazing heights. When asked to pick the top techniques to help reach your goals in business, he said that you should begin by setting out what your goals are, and then writing them down. He said you should also be clear on why you want to reach them and make plans and decisions while keeping your goals in mind. Then build a strategy and have an ironclad focus and determination to get there.

He also reaffirmed that people and relationships are paramount. In his mind, it all comes down to people, from business partners and clients to your employees. For business partners, you must agree on a vision, ensure you understand each other's commitment, make sure your skill sets add value to your overall goals, and you must have respect for each other.

For clients, Pat says that people do business with who they know and like, but of course you also need to have the service or product to back it up. With regard to your employees, Pat says you should never ask them to do something you would not do yourself and that it is your role as leader to support them every way you can, make the time to talk with them, and truly understand their point of view. I agree with Pat when he says that leadership comes in many forms and there is no cookie-cutter template to imitate. People follow leaders who are genuine.

The third highly successful and inspirational business person whom I asked for a profile is Jimmie Inch. Jimmie wears so many hats, it's hard to describe everything he does, but right now, he is an entrepreneur, structural engineer, musician, and business coach. I like Jimmie's approach because it is down to earth and very practical.

He is at the stage in his life where he has built his engineering business to the point that he has time to pursue his many other passions and businesses, which is truly inspirational. Jimmie doesn't see a big difference between personal and business goals and he usually just calls them life goals.

Jimmie says when someone comes to him looking for a change out of lack or out of a negative situation, he first recommends that they take a month to get in touch with their body, mind and spirit. He says they should begin to eat right if they are not already doing so, and focus on real whole foods, mostly vegetables, and drink only water for a month. He is a strong proponent of daily exercise and recommends that everyone do at least 30 minutes of physical exercise of some kind every day.

Jimmie also says it is necessary to meditate each day but that can take any number of forms, including walking quietly through nature or simply following a meditation practice that they like. Jimmie also feels that it is important to be part of a group of like-minded people. According to him, this is necessary because we are a social species and he feels that being part of a group where we can share interests and ideas with others is a big part of leading a fulfilled life. Jimmie says it can be as simple as joining a book club, playing on a sports team, coaching a team, or playing in a band. In terms of business groups, he recommends that people start or join a mastermind group and I can attest that he is an excellent person to mastermind with, since I previously attended a mastermind group with him.

Jimmie says that it's a mistake to make major life decisions without first giving one's mind and body a reset for month because a person is able to make better decisions and set appropriate goals only once they've reached a state of clarity.

Now it's time for you to *Doyle It In* and try out the last three exercises which will help you improve your time management skills, keep your vision in sight, and track your daily actions in a practical way. After that I'm offering a brief conclusion and some additional valuable resources that I highly recommend you read over, to get the full picture of this whole transformational process.

Doyle It In Exercise #13:

Improve Your Daily Productivity

This exercise introduces four ways that you can develop habits to improve your daily performance and achieve your goals faster.

You may have heard of some of these before, or similar ideas, but the focus today is for you to choose something to take action on and actually try it out.

1. **Set Your Intention:** Set your intention for the day as soon as possible upon waking up and you will find that you can run your day rather than having your day run you. I like to write my intention for the day out in pen, as I find this is a good way to ensure that I work on the priority tasks that will get me to my goals in the best way.

2. **Improve Your Time Management:** I can't hammer this home enough. It is absolutely critical to work on just one thing at a time. Manage your time so you can do focused work on your priority items without distraction. Personally, I highly recommend that you create and use a form similar to the Project 101 Taking Action Work Sheet Template which I'm going to tell you more about in Exercise # 15 below, so you can organize the things you need to get done in any given day, week and month.

3. **Schedule in Short Breaks**: Remember to take time between projects or tasks to reboot, walk around, or have a glass of water before changing gears toward the next task. One way is to split your work day into sections of no more than 60 minutes at a time and then take about 5 to 10 minutes to either have a break or transition in some way before heading into the next task. This will increase your productivity significantly even if you plan on working on the same item for several hours in a row. I learned this technique from author Brendon Burchard and I have found it really effective.

4. ***Brain Dump Regularly***: Many of you may have heard of a "brain dump" but the importance of doing this regularly is really important and therefore bears repeating. Our brains are not really meant to hoard everything but rather to process our thoughts and ideas. In order to clear your brain, take these brain dumping steps on a regular basis: write things down, sort through them, prioritize them, and then plan when you will work on each item. Once you get the jumble of tasks out of your head and organized, your brain can then get back to processing each item in its turn. I learned a very similar process from Christine Kane. It was a bonus course called, *"Uplevel Your Productivity."*

Now that I've explained these four techniques, it's your turn to think about how you can apply them in your daily life. Here are a few questions to get started.

1. Of these four ideas I have listed above, are there any you already follow? If yes, list which ones.

2. If these are new techniques to you, which sound good to you and why?

3. Are there any ideas listed above that you feel resistance about? If yes, explain why?

4. Do you feel that over time you can begin to implement these habits into your daily routine?

Think about which new time management habit you are willing to begin to implement now so that you can improve your performance and profitability, and ultimately achieve your goals sooner. Commit to trying at least one strategy each day over the next week, and then expand your practice to a second, third or fourth idea each week during the next month. Track your completion rate on your work to see which techniques work best for you and tweak these ideas in your own way if that suits you better.

Doyle It In Exercise #14:

Keep Your Vision in Sight

Gone are the days of setting long-term goals. I know this might sound strange, but give me a minute and I think it will start to make sense. As humans, we are creatures of habit and we are programmed to love the feeling of *completion*. When we set a goal that is too broad in scope, or too far away in time, we can quickly lose momentum. That is because we don't see the cumulative effect of our daily actions until months and months down the road.

Within this exercise, I'd like to suggest that you try the system I use and see if it will work for you. My vision and bigger picture is long term but I no longer set goals that are longer than 3 months in duration. This slight change allows me to continue to move the needle toward the bigger picture, but I get to feel a great sense of accomplishment at least every quarter.

In addition to this, within each 3-month quarterly cycle, I recommend that you set several touch points where tasks and projects can be completed on route to achieving your overall quarterly goals. That way you will experience the rewarding feeling of completion several times before each goal is completed.

Before starting Exercise 15 coming up, I ask you to take some time now to think about your current goals and clearly identify what your overall vision is. Once you have your vision established, break down what steps, actions and projects must take place to make this vision a reality. I believe you will begin to see that separate goals will start to reveal themselves and that's great. Now you have a lead-in to the project worksheet that is included in Exercise 15 below.

Once you start to build these highly effective habits and do this planning every quarter, you will find that your clarity on any given day will be crystal clear. I am confident you can rock this section out of the park and dramatically reduce the feelings of overwhelm compared to when you might just be trying to wing it. I believe you can do it, and I am excited to find out where these systems and increased clarity take you.

Doyle It In Exercise #15:

Sort and Track Your Priority Projects

As a final exercise think of a project you've perhaps been wanting to tackle but which has you feeling overwhelmed, or use one of the ones that you worked out in Exercise 14. Now, try to break it out into bite size steps or action items, because as we said above, we all like the feeling of *completion* and longer term goals can feel daunting. So, let your vision be long-term while setting shorter term goals, ones that can be achievable in 12 weeks or less.

I encourage you to use the Project 101 *Taking Action Work Sheet Template* form (which I have included in Valuable Resources Section #6) to start planning your next project or work assignment. To work with this chart, write the name of each project or assignment under the heading "Project #". The eight rows under each project are where you will write down your action items in the order they need to happen to complete each smaller step in the overall project.

Please note there may only be 2 or 3 actions items for certain projects and more than 8 for some others. This is a simple table to build on and it's meant to streamline your projects into an efficient workflow. I use this too I often because it gives me instant visual clarity.

Since this concept might be new to you, here's an example of how this form can work to keep actions on track and moving forward. When I was working on the planning and running of the music festival up North, I started by itemizing what gear I needed and who I needed to contact for what. I entered the info for each contact person or company in first column along with what I thought they could do for us, and then I wrote out what steps I would use to contact them, depending on how well I knew them.

I took time at the beginning to carefully work out the best way to communicate with all the potential sponors, funders, community partners, venues, and the Festival committee and president. When seeking to get a hold of the necessary gear for example, for the people I knew very well and I was asking for something relatively simple, I planned just a quick phone call to ask for help.

But for other larger businesses and sponsors that I didn't know as well, my tasks on the *Project 101 Template* form included four initial action items: first action item was that I would put the specific request to that company in writing for their consideration; second action item was that I would call the general office number to double check who the request should be addressed to in the company; third action item was to add the person's name and title to the request, and then send the request by mail or email; and the fourth action item was to follow up in one week. Additional follow ups or meetings were scheduled if there was not an immediate decision by the company. Every day for the first month, I worked this list and used the form to track answers and additional steps until we had access to all the gear and donations that we needed.

I organized the *Stagehand Scheduling* in a similar way on a separate *Project 101 Template* form, and included as the first action item the task of creating a standard letter to give to each stagehand so they would be clear about the exact duties and responsibilities, what hours they would be needed for, and what they would be paid, so that everyone would know this was a professional paid gig and not just a personal favour to me.

After that, I created several other *Project 101 Template* forms for other individual parts of the bigger project such as *Marketing and Media Activities, Tracking Budget Criteria, Venue Checks and Prep*, and so on.

I encourage you to try out the *Project 101 Taking Action Work Sheet Template* to outline and track the action steps for your next project or work assignment to see how it works for you. Again, you can adjust the way you work with the form so it complements your own situation, or customize it for yourself, whatever works best.

CONCLUSION

We are never stuck in life. We may feel stuck from time to time but the world is made up of energy and is always moving and changing. It is our thoughts that we get stuck in. Once you change your thoughts, mindset and actions, you begin to create a different result.

The Serenity Prayer really helped me when I felt at my lowest and was looking to make big changes. I know now the importance of accepting the things I cannot change, having the courage to change the things I can, and the wisdom to know the difference. I realize now that moving forward is not always about making a quantum leap; instead it's made up of small manageable daily changes that make a massive difference over time.

By our very nature, we tend to overestimate what we can do in a short period while drastically underestimating what we can do over a long period. The fact that you are reading this book, that it got written and published, proves that this system works.

I fully admit that writing this book was my most daunting project to date. My success in completing it is directly linked to using all the tools mentioned in the five Pillars.

There are a lot of books out there covering specific areas of life for healing or personal growth. My intention was to cover many different areas with reference to specific resources, so you can take whatever path to healing and self-discovery that you need in order to grow, heal and live fully. I hope the tools and advice provided will aid in unlocking your full potential as you move forward.

Continuous self-investment really increases your chances of staying motivated and enjoying life in general. I don't know all the answers, but I am confident that the contents of this book, when implemented, can make a positive impact on your quality of life. I say this because I have written it from a place of passion, love and an authentic desire to help as many people as possible to improve their lives on many levels.

There is no such thing as failure. There are only outcomes that you can learn from as you move forward. Let the obstacles you face become opportunities for you to grow. I fully believe in you, so as you continue on your life's journey, always be your authentic self, believe in yourself and shine your amazing light.

You're going to rock it!

VALUABLE
RESOURCES

#1 – A COMMON SENSE APPROACH TO HEALTHY EATING

This section contains my common sense approach to healthy eating. I like to share this widely because these techniques have improved my mental clarity and elevated my mood and energy on a daily basis.

Nutrition is something that can be improved over time, one day at a time. With so much information out there on different diets and "what to do and what not to do," many people whom I talk to admit to being confused and overwhelmed. The good news is it doesn't have to be complicated nor do you need to try to change everything at once. Actually, real sustainable change comes from slowly changing one thing at a time and building habits until they make their way into your natural routines.

I am not a nutritionist but I know what works for me and what has worked for so many other people. I am happy to share the following general guidelines and tips for grocery shopping, as well as how to prepare and eat healthy whole foods.

There is no secret grocery list or group of recipes that yields amazing results for everyone. We are all different and have different lifestyles and unique needs. But what we have in common, in my opinion, is that everyone needs a healthy portion of all the macronutrients and micronutrients in order to function at an optimum level.

Personally I don't really like all the "fad diets" out there because most of them are about reducing or eliminating certain things from our diet. These diets do have some positive things in common like advising to reduce processed foods, eat in moderation, eat mindfully and drink enough water.

General Guidelines for Healthy Eating

So let me start with some general guidelines on healthy eating:

- Eat whole foods.
- Drink 8 to 10 glasses of water daily.
- Don't skip breakfast.
- Combine lean protein and complex carbohydrates with every meal.
- Eat produce that is in season.
- Eat smaller amounts more frequently (4-6 meals daily).
- Eat slowly and mindfully.
- Ensure you get enough healthy fats.
- Eat 8 to 10 servings of veggies a day.
- Ensure you eat a variety of healthy foods to maximize your nutritional intake.

Grocery Shopping and Making Meals

Here are some general guidelines for grocery shopping and preparing food that virtually anyone can do:

- Walk mostly around the perimeter of the grocery store because that is where the fresh produce, dairy products, and meats are located.
- Stay away from the inside grocery aisles that are stacked with processed foods.
- When reading the ingredients, avoid products that have too many items listed and are hard to even pronounce.
- Slowly develop the habit of planning and preparing healthy meals on the weekends so that you can enjoy them all week.
- Always prepare extra so you can have healthy snacks.
- Buy a good set of sealable containers that will keep your food fresh.
- Pack a cooler or lunch bag daily to stay on track and be fueled with healthy food all day.
- Learn to order healthy choices when eating out.
- Be ready to clean the slate when you go off track and return to healthier eating.
- Focus on the positive changes you are making rather than worrying about the things you haven't changed yet or the pizza you ate at a work luncheon.
- Treat yourself to one or two special meals a week but in moderation (preferably on the same set of days weekly).

Clean Eating and Whole Foods

As you develop clean eating habits, you will slowly become more in tune with what your body needs. I believe over time you will start to crave the healthier foods more often than the burger or slice of pizza. I am not saying you will never feel like a burger or pizza, but it will happen less often. I still enjoy my few slices of pizza every Saturday but now, much more often, I crave the clean foods and the energy they provide for my body.

Please keep in mind that I didn't just wake up one morning and say, "Okay, it's time to change all my current bad nutritional habits and eat clean from now on." I took small steps, changing one thing at a time until it became a new habit. You can do it too. There are several theories on how long it takes to develop a new habit but what is important is that you work on being as consistent as possible. Before you know it, healthy eating will become a seamless part of your daily routine and lifestyle.

Defining the Terms

Clean eating has been a buzzword in the world of fitness and nutrition for a while now but it's certainly not something new. Elite athletes and bodybuilders have been using clean eating to fuel their training and help them achieve their goals for years. Clean eating means consciously choosing whole foods or real foods. *Whole foods* are basically foods that are as close to their natural state as possible like root vegetables, fresh fruits, leafy greens, and lean unprocessed meats.

Taking time to plan your week of meals on the weekend and prepare your meals in advance may seem hard at first but again, over time, it will become routine. This routine really increases how well you eat and it improves your daily energy levels. When you commit to whole foods, you select these over *processed food*. The food processing industry has not been around for that long when we look at human history. Although diets have varied depending on where you lived in the world, humans ate mostly natural whole foods until about 100 years ago.

There are many good resources on the topic of clean eating, but one author I really enjoy is Tosca Reno. She has written several great books on how to adopt an eat clean diet. Her books really helped me slowly clean up my nutritional habits and those new habits have been with me for more than five years now. What I like is that her books read well, are not too heavy or technical, and her passion and energy for this topic is very evident in her writing. She also has several great recipe books including "The Eat-Clean Diet for Men."

A Few Words About Supplements

I don't consider myself an expert on supplements, but with so much information out there and the fact that there is little to no regulation within this industry, I feel that supplements are worth a brief discussion. I personally feel there is no replacement for eating healthy whole foods. However, supplements can add additional value.

Even when trying to eat clean and avoid processed food, you still may not always get the quality nutrients in certain foods that you would have not so long ago. This is due to many factors including increased pollution and the fact that the systems and approaches sometimes used for growing certain foods can lead to lower nutritional values than you might want or expect. And of course, if you are very physically active and workout regularly, there is value in taking certain types of supplements.

I believe everyone can benefit from taking a high quality multi-vitamin. I also personally use protein powder, branched chain amino acids (BCAAs), and creatine. Additional "fat burners" like green tea extract and CLA can help when used in conjunction with good nutrition and exercise but are not required and are simply a personal choice.

Depending on my fitness goals I have used various supplements and products from time to time and found them helpful. Obviously I would suggest that you consult your doctor before taking any of the supplements I've mentioned.

Tracking and Counting

Counting calories can have a place and add value for reaching a specific goal but I don't feel that counting calories is natural and people can sometimes get really obsessed with this process. In my six years of doing a strict fitness regime and getting more and more into nutrition, I have only tracked my calories for two weeks. I felt there was value in doing it just that brief time to get a handle on what I was eating, but overall there are some better techniques for tracking the foods you are eating.

Toward that end, I do recommend keeping a food journal when you are trying to fine-tune your nutrition and learn what works best for you. A food journal isn't really a big time commitment and you have a reference to see what you ate when you had a high performance day or a great workout or when you had a down day or a not-so-great workout. A food journal can also quickly identify possible gaps in your diet.

I kept a food journal for several months and it helped me slowly add more variety to my diet, specifically adding more greens. Although I haven't kept a food journal for well over two years, I could see myself doing it again on occasion depending on my specific fitness goals in the future. Tracking your food choices with a food journal can help weed out bad habits that may have crept in without you noticing.

I hope the main take-home message that you get from this overview on nutrition is that we are all different and what works for you might not work for the next person. It's all about making positive changes, one step at a time, and finding out what is best for you over time.

#2 – A COMMON SENSE APPROACH TO FITNESS

Thank you for checking out this section where I share my take on fitness based on my personal experience. This is an overview with some of the insights I learned over time about fitness and how I have made it work for me. I have been able to drastically improve my strength, body composition, and capacity to work toward other goals in life.

There is a natural connection between fitness and nutrition. As you become more knowledgeable about both, I think you will come to realize, as I have, that fitness cannot help you overcome a poor diet, but if you ensure that your workouts are fueled efficiently with good nutrition, the combination can yield amazing results.

General Guidelines for Fitness

When it comes to fitness, there are general guidelines you can follow. The following list is intended to form a starting point and then you can fine-tune as required based on your personal needs and the goals you set. Remember you should consult a doctor before taking up your intended fitness activities to ensure your body and general health are OK to begin such a regime.

- Ensure that you do some dynamic stretching and warm up pre-workout and a cool down and static stretch post-workout.
- Try being active for 30 minutes daily which can include walking, hiking, jogging, biking, going to the gym or doing other physical activities.
- Strength train at least 2 to 3 days a week if you want to build muscle and maintain bone density (this is increasingly important as you get older).
- Ensure your body is getting enough recovery time.
- Do mobility work at least 3 to 4 days a week (foam roller, stretching, yoga, and so on).
- Ensure you are getting 7 to 9 hours of rest a night.

In my opinion, every aspect of life requires balance and it is best to make gradual improvements toward your goals. I believe there is value in aerobic activity, high intensity training, weight training, yoga, and many other physical activities and sports. If you want to have good mobility and functional strength, then a balanced approach is required.

Benefits of Physical Activity

Some benefits of regular physical activity are as follows:

- Increased energy and elevated mood.
- Lower blood pressure.
- Increased lung capacity.
- Higher metabolism.
- Increased lean muscle mass.
- Increased fat loss.
- Increased chances of a much longer life span.
- Reduced stress.
- More confidence.
- Improved appearance.
- Increased bone density.

The feeling you get from being active is much more than a physical change. There is a major mind-body-spirit connection that is magnified when you are good to your body, mind and soul. I fully believe you will see increased personal growth if you take the time to be good to yourself and eat well while being active.

Setting Up a Fitness Training Plan

How you structure your fitness training should be based on your experience, current fitness level, goals, and mobility level. The science of structuring an effective workout program can get very technical and involves various principles and approaches. For example, the Frequency, Intensity, Time and Type (FITT) principle covers how often you train, at what level of intensity, over what time period, and the type of training you do.

Professional athletes use periodized programs when they train, but should a non-athlete use this method of training? I would say, most definitely, yes! It will reduce the chance of injury, limit plateaus, and get you to your goals in the most timely, safe, and effective way possible.

A basic cycle during a periodized program could be as follows:

- Foundation.
- Build.
- Burn.
- Strength.

Foundation: The main purpose of a foundation phase is to teach correct movement patterns and reduce the chance of injury. This phase is in alignment with Functional Movement System's theory of first move well, then move often. Any muscle imbalances and asymmetries that are present during the primal movements (squat, lunge, bend, twist, push and pull) can be corrected here before moving on to the build phase. A solid foundation is imperative to safely and successfully achieve your fitness goals. I find this phase really improves your movement and posture, making day-to-day chores easier.

Build: The main focus of a build phase is to add lean muscle mass. Every pound of lean muscle you gain will burn up to 50 to 100 extra calories a day. Lean muscle will increase your metabolism and help burn fat. In this phase, you would usually perform the primal movements only weighted. You will quite likely find that this phase also improves your quality of sleep.

Burn: The main focus in a burn phase is to shed fat. This is one of my favorite phases as it releases the feel good endorphins. In the burn phase, you would perform circuits, HIIT and possibly weight lifting with a cardio effect.

Strength: The main focus of a strength phase is to increase your strength. Two of the best predictors in life expectancy are your lean muscle mass and your strength levels. This phase is really demanding on your central nervous system and adequate rest is imperative. You would be lifting heavy weights within a low rep range and allow longer rest in-between sets. When you make sure you get a good sleep and have a recovery system in place, this phase will help increase your fitness gains. I also find that this phase brings awesome mental clarity.

I won't get into further detail on the different types of workouts or training methods but you can find out more advice and workouts on websites like: "EatToPerform.com" and "BodyBuilding.com".

Working with a Personal Trainer

Just as an additional reminder, I would strongly suggest that before starting any type of workout regime, you consult your doctor for advice and approval. I would also recommend if you really want to maximize your time and efforts in the gym toward a specific goal, hire a personal trainer.

Working with a personal trainer can have several advantages such as:

- You will feel more accountable.
- You get support and motivation to keep you on track.
- You reduce the chance of injury.
- You get an individualized training regime to efficiently work towards your specific goals.

When looking for a trainer, ensure you do your homework and ask lots of questions. As in many other fields of work, there are great trainers and not-so-great trainers out there.

Look for the following points when selecting a trainer:

- Their certifications are up to date.
- They walk the talk and are in great shape themselves.
- They are energetic.
- They are passionate about fitness.
- They are good listeners (trainers who listen tend to design more effective programs).
- They are genuinely interested in helping and motivating you.

It has been statistically shown that a trainer will get you to your goals up to three times faster than doing it on your own. I would have to say that in most cases when we really look at our spending habits, most people can make adjustments and manage to afford a trainer. It really comes back to self- investment and the acceptance that without your health, you will not be able to live fully while serving others. Instead of thinking, "I can't afford to pay for training," ask yourself, "Can I afford not to?"

This being said, if you can't afford a trainer you can still get results. In this case, I often suggest finding a workout partner. Certain people need that extra push to remain motivated and stay on track. If you tell a friend you'll meet them at 6 a.m. for a morning run, you are more likely to follow through because someone else is depending on you. Another advantage in having a workout buddy is you will generally work harder than if you were just running or working out on your own.

I am quite certain that when you make time for fitness, you will become more productive and happier than if you don't take the time. Without your health, nothing else really matters. In order to enjoy life, thrive, and be there for your loved ones, you need your health and strength.

I hope the main take-home message that you get from this overview is that we are all different and what works for you might not work for the next person. It's all about making positive changes and finding out what is best for you over time.

#3 – INSPIRATIONAL SUCCESS TIPS: MAUREEN (MO) HAGAN

Maureen (Mo) Hagan - Vice President, Program Innovation and Fitness Development. Goodlife Fitness.

In her own words: My name is Maureen (Mo) Hagan and I've been a "goal-getter" as long as I can remember. Since I was a young girl I always dreamed of becoming a physiotherapist so that I could help people exercise and learn how to care for their health. I was inspired by my high-school physical education teacher who first introduced me to fitness. She taught me that, if I wanted to achieve something I would need to set a goal, and work hard until I achieved it. She taught me how to focus on specific and measureable daily actions that were relevant to my goal, realistic to my abilities and according to deadline. Most importantly she showed me how to actualize having achieved the goal even before I had.

Although I was not the most gifted student or athlete in my school, I practiced and worked harder than most of the other students, and through goal setting, I learned to believe anything was possible.

I knew my life purpose was to teach and inspire people through exercise and I envisioned in my mind that I would travel the world and teach and train in a new model of health care. While I was told by my guidance counsellor there was no such career as the one I was imagining (which there wasn't in 1979), I was bold enough to ask questions, challenge the status quo, seek mentorship and work hard in pursuit of my dreams, despite the many roadblocks along my journey. Who said that success was a straight road anyway?

I was determined so I set my mind on reaching this career goal and even before I knew the amazing power of goal setting, I simply acted on passion, on knowing my purpose and I unleashed its power. Following a degree in Physical Health Education, I returned to school and became a physiotherapist. I worked in a large teaching hospital and at the same time, I pursued my passion in fitness as a group fitness instructor.

As a licensed physiotherapist and award-winning fitness professional, I have been travelling the world since 1991 helping to shape and lead the fitness industry. I have been blessed with many great opportunities to serve others and be recognized for my achievements. My success and deep desire to shape self-care through a world of motion drives me to continue on my journey of goal setting.

I have invested in personal development and coaching and I continue to do so. It is one of the most important and worthwhile investments I have made in my life. I encourage anybody who wants to be successful, in any area of life, to read self-development books and find a mentor, or work with a coach.

Everything you do starts with belief, belief shapes your attitude, and attitude shifts your thoughts. Your thoughts shape your words and your words lead your actions. With ongoing self-development, you will develop the strength that will help protect your thoughts and attitude, help build your self-belief and help you master your actions.

You will also acquire healthy and masterful principles, reference points and habits that will help lead you in the direction of your goals and on your path to success. To ensure I'm heading in the right direction in my journey, I carry my goals in my wallet and they have become my affirmations that I can verbalize, visualize and meditate upon multiple times per day.

As the self-made millionaire, success coach, and philosopher Jim Rohn would say, "You want to set a goal that is big enough that in the process of achieving it, you become someone worth becoming." Each one of us is worth becoming someone great.

My Three Most Important Tips in Goal Setting:

1. Begin with a success mindset that you have already achieved your goal and then follow through with daily and disciplined action in pursuit of that goal.

2. Protect your beliefs, attitude and thoughts from those who may not support your dream.

3. Verbalize and visualize your goal each morning. Act as if you have achieved it (make it real) and then reflect each evening on your progress.

#4 – INSPIRATIONAL SUCCESS TIPS: PATRICK DOYLE

Patrick Doyle, CEO & Founding Partner, Scarlet Security & Risk Group (SSRG)

In his own words: My name is Patrick Doyle and I'm happy to write up some details about my career at the request of my brother, Michael. He asked me to give you some of my personal background in the job I do and share some information about how I use goal setting and other principles each day.

As a business owner, investor, and consultant over the years, I have worked in many different industries always with an emphasis on strategic opportunities with a focus on collaborations. These have included, identifying new market verticals for strategic targets that fit the abilities of a corporation, identifying, and developing strategic partnerships to pursue those opportunities, always factoring the importance of local stakeholder engagement for overall success.

In terms of my personal journey in business, early in my career I was focused getting to the answer as fast as possible, I read book after book on management and would read anything I could get my hands on. Management is highly focused on systems, processes and that the inputs will dictate outputs. These are important in a corporate environment, and we have great process people in our organization. I've shifted a large part of my time to leadership, which requires a much more nuanced approach as your dealing with people.

The practice of mindfulness would also be a large part of my evolve as a Leader. It has become a large part of focus over the years and one I would contribute many positives outcomes and results we're realized as a group. It has helped in so many parts of my life and business, yet it is still very much a work in progress.

I will always remain wholeheartedly committed to my belief that the greatest strength of any company is the people in it.

Further to the people in our company identifying and cultivating a join vision with the right industry partners to be successful with and grow together is of equal importance. We build strong long-term partnerships built on mutual trust and respect in the communities we operate. Scarlet now has many indigenous equity partnerships, and we have and will continue to see great success in doing so. We truly believe that their success is also our company's success.

Getting into this current business, I was appointed as President of Scarlet Security in 2006 and I moved to Yellowknife NWT. The company flourished and in 2012, I continued to growth the company and became the majority owner and CEO of Scarlet Security Group in 2015.

As the CEO, my role has been to be the driving force in expanding the company's assets in Western Canada and in forming and maintaining strategic relationships with owner- clients and community stakeholders. More importantly we've been able to build a leadership team to take on large, complex integrated programs and has placed us on unique footing for the future.

Building a true leadership team has really taken us to new highs. The company has moved into new stages such as integrating many cutting-edge technologies as part of a larger commitment to deliver value-added services. This has all been part of the natural evolution and growing trend toward the merger of security services, risk and technology.

I work along with our leadership team to set the corporation's strategy and vision and try to ensure that our strategic direction guides and informs our decision-making, while still ensuring that within our corporate culture, everyone feels engaged and wants to continue to be a part of it.

In offering advice to other leaders, I would say that it's important for your team to believe in both the message and the messenger. There are of course other important factors such as building and leading an executive team that is not just ready for today but fully set for where your vision is taking you. I recommend that you provide your group with the resources to do their jobs and you let smart people do what they do, as long as it continues to fit with the overall company values and priorities.

When I bought the company with my business partner in 2015, we were a profitable well-run northern company.

My vision was to take our northern model and move into larger contracts outside of the north. But I wanted to do it by using the same model we had first developed in the north, whereby we really focused on highly tailored services and higher levels of training and greater awareness of our employees. We also worked closely with First Nations and were able to set up meaningful partnerships to provide security to large industrial environments.

At the time in 2015, Scarlet had one First Nation partnership and one Inuit partnership, and all operations were in the NWT and Nunavut. Four years later, we were able to successfully expand that model to the point where Scarlet Security, which is still a 100% Canadian-owned corporation, now operates many

Aboriginal partnership corporations and J-Vs (joint ventures) in the Northwest Territories, Nunavut, Alberta, British Columbia, and Saskatchewan. These companies provide a full suite of security services to Governments, LNG, oil and gas, pipeline and mining industries, and many other large environments.

Important Elements in Goal Setting

There are so many key elements that help people reach amazing heights. A few that come to mind are: drive and shear will, focus, direction, flexibility, the ability to relentlessly work your network, being adaptable, the ability to self- evaluate, being willing to surround yourself with positive smart people, the capacity to let go at the right times and establishing business processes to make them systemic and scalable.

If I had to pick 3 key elements to help reach your goals in business, they would be as follows:

1. Set what your goals are and write them down. If you don't where you're going, you will never get there. Give thought to why you want to reach them and make plans and decisions keeping your goals in mind. Build a strategy and have an ironclad focus and determination to get there.

2. People and relationships are paramount. It all comes down to people, from your leadership team and clients to your employees. For your leadership team, you must agree on a overall vision, ensure you understand each other's commitments, make sure your skill sets add value to your overall goals, and you must have respect for each other. For clients, remember that people do business with who they know and like, but then you also need the service or product to back it up, and you need the right people in the right roles at the right time within your operations. You want your client's trust and loyalty, and money cannot buy those. Trust and loyalty are developed over time by living up to your word and building a reputation for reliability. With regard to your employees, never ask them to do something you would not do yourself. Support them every way you can and make the time to talk with them and understand their point of view. Put yourself in their shoes. Leadership comes in many forms and there is no cookie-cutter template to imitate. People follow leaders who are genuine.

3. Always want more but for the right reasons. For me, in business, it's the love of the deal. You should always take the time to enjoy your wins but it's the getting up early the next day with as much or more drive for the next task that takes you to new levels. Be grateful for where

you are and don't forget the important lessons that you learned and the experiences that helped shape you as a person over the years. Remember the original approach that got you where you are, and don't lose the hunger.

#5 – INSPIRATIONAL SUCCESS TIPS: JIMMIE INCH

Jimmie Inch – Entrepreneur, Structural Engineer, Musician, TV Host & Business Coach.

In his own words: My name is Jimmie Inch and I'm a 44-year- old happily married father of three and a grandfather of one. I started young. I usually have difficulty describing what I do for a living given the vast number of fields I have worked in.

I am a structural engineer by trade and I own a small firm in eastern Canada. I am fortunate that I have built that business to the point where I have time for my other passions and businesses. I am a long-time musician, I hosted a nationally syndicated radio show for 10 years, and I spent the last four years also producing and hosting three regional TV shows via the production company that I own. I am also a certified coach and in the last few years I have also taken on clients as a business and entrepreneurial coach.

While I am fortunate to have achieved many business and personal goals I have set for myself, I am always setting new goals and working towards them. I personally don't see a big difference between personal and business goals so I usually just call them life goals.

Often, when I am dealing with a client who wants to set new goals for themselves, I find that the desire to change some aspect of their life comes from a place of lack. Maybe their business is failing, maybe they are in a relationship that isn't working, or maybe their health isn't at a level where they want it to be. There is usually some area of their life that is lacking that has triggered the desire to change. The opposite of this would be somebody looking to grow an already successful business, someone looking to take a personal relationship to the next level, or somebody who is excelling in fitness but has set a new personal goal.

The Best Way to Approach Goal Setting

Whenever I feel that someone is looking for a change out of lack or a negative situation, here is what I recommend they do before they make any major life decisions. Take a month to do the following:

1. Eat right. – While this seems like an oversimplification, it is a key component to a healthy, successful life. I recommend that they eat real whole foods, mostly vegetables, and drink only water for a month. New studies have shown the link between gut bacteria and

forms of depression and energy levels. I won't go into it here but I would recommend that if you are interested, pick up a copy of *The Good Gut* by Drs Justin and Erica Sonnenburg of Stanford University. It's a real eye-opener.

2. Exercise daily. – Again, it sounds cliché but I am shocked at the number of people who don't exercise daily. I recommend that everyone do at least 30 minutes of physical exercise of some kind every day. I consider daily physical exercise a must in order to maximize your life.

3. Meditate daily. – I feel that everyone should do some form of meditation every day. That said, the best type of meditation varies from person to person. Some people may use prayer, some may surf, some may go for a walk in the woods, and some may simply follow a meditation practice. For those new to meditation, I usually recommend starting with the *Headspace* app for smart phones. It's a great introduction into meditation. Currently, I am following the Wim Hof Method of breathing which has been a game changer for me. To learn more about Wim Hof, I usually recommend that people watch the Vice mini-documentary, "Inside the Superhuman World of the Iceman", which is available free on YouTube.

4. Be part of a group of like-minded people. – This is advice that usually takes people by surprise but I believe it is very important. We are a social species and I think being part of a group where we can share interests and ideas is a big part of leading a fulfilled life for most people. This can be as simple as joining a book club, playing on a sports team, coaching a team, or playing in a band. In terms of business groups, I recommend people start or

join a mastermind group which is essentially a regularly scheduled conference call where people can share ideas.

I feel that if a person follows the above four recommendations for a month, they are then in a much better position to proceed to set new goals and start taking action towards those goals. I think it is a mistake to make major life decisions without first giving one's mind and body a reset for a month. A person is able to make better decisions when they've reached a state of clarity.

Lastly, once the month is over and they are ready to start setting new goals and taking action, I introduce them to journaling. I am a firm believer that writing down daily and long-term goals, as well as documenting progress, are key steps in efficiently achieving goals.

#6 – PROJECT 101 TAKING ACTION WORK SHEET TEMPLATE

To work with this chart, write the name of each project under the Project #.

The eight rows under each project are where you will write down your action items in the order, they need to happen to complete each project.

Please note there may only be 2-3 actions items for certain projects and more than 8 for others. It's a simple table to build on and it's meant to streamline your projects into an efficient workflow. I use this often and like that it provides instant visual clarity.

Project #1	Project #2

You can download a full-sized copy of my work sheet template at www. atthehelm.us/resources

#7 – QUICK LIST OF *DOYLE IT IN* EXERCISES

Doyle It In Exercise #1: *Create Your Own Vision Board*

Doyle It In Exercise #2: *Become Clear on Your Core Desires*

Doyle It In Exercise #3: *Set Your Initial Intentions*

Doyle It In Exercise #4: *Tap Into Your Inner Energy and Wisdom*

Doyle It In Exercise #5: *Get to Know Your Obstacles and Fears*

Doyle It In Exercise #6: *Overcome Your Obstacles and Fears*

Doyle It In Exercise #7: *Disconnect to Reconnect*

Doyle It In Exercise #8: *Be Thankful Every Day*

Doyle It In Exercise #9: *Find Ways to Give to Others Daily*

Doyle It In Exercise #10: *Become Better at Self-care*

Doyle It In Exercise #11: *Create Your Own Circle of Influence*

Doyle It In Exercise #12: *Build Your Own Solid Foundation and Set New Goals*

Doyle It In Exercise #13: *Improve Your Daily Productivity*

Doyle It In Exercise #14: *Keep Your Vision in Sight*

Doyle It In Exercise #15: *Sort and Track Your Priority Projects*

#8 – SUGGESTED REFERENCES & EXPERTS

#8 – Suggested References & Experts

Christine Kane
christinekane.com
info@uplevelyou.com

Christine Kane is President and Founder of Uplevel YOU™, a million-dollar company that propels purpose-driven entrepreneurs into the highest level of their business and lifestyle success.

Sandy Levey Lunden
www.sandylevey.com
onpurpose@sandylevey.com

Sandy Levey Lunden's special brand of coaching has helped clients reconcile with their spouses, rekindle relationships with absent fathers, renew loving, permanent connection with domineering mothers and re-establish productive, rewarding careers.

Brendon Burchard
www.brendonburchard.com
support@brendon.com

Brendon Burchard is the world's leading high performance coach and one of the most-watched, quoted and followed personal development trainers in history.

John Berardi
www.precisionnutrition.com
info@precisionnutrition.com

John Berardi, PhD, CSCS is Co-Founder of Precision Nutrition. He has devoted his entire career to making health and fitness something that's achievable and attainable for every type of person, from every walk of life.

Jim Rohn
www.jimrohn.com/
customersupport@jimrohn.com

JimRohn.com was launched in 1997 and is the official website of Jim Rohn (1930-2009), America's foremost authority on success, world- renowned business philosopher, and a recognized legend in the fields of motivation and personal achievement.

Nate Green
nategreen.org

Nate Green is a fitness writer and author who shares ways to simplify your health and fitness, improve your focus, and earn your freedom.

Tosca Reno
toscareno.com/tosca

Tosca Reno's passion for championing the Eat-Clean lifestyle began when she took control of her life and transformed her body from being overweight to strong and fit at age 40

Hal Elrod
Halelrod.com

Hal Elrod is a #1 best-selling author and the creator of *The Miracle Morning* book series. He is also a Hall of Fame business achiever, renowned keynote speaker, and an ultra-marathon runner.

ACKNOWLEDGMENTS

It has been an amazing adventure from the seed of this book being planted to seeing it come into full fruition. I want to first thank Jimmie Inch for planting this seed in the first place. I can instantly go back to the time when we talked on the phone. I was sitting at my desk at Aboriginal Affairs and Northern Development and decided to call Jimmie on my coffee break. I shared with Jimmie my ideas on fitness and nutrition and my plan to get into the health and wellness industry. He said, "I think you should write a book. Based on what you were telling me, it sounds like a book to me." I must admit that at the time I didn't see myself as a writer. However, something about that idea really resonated with me. I was in an inspiring state energetically and was open to the possibilities. Thank you, Jimmie, for your encouragement and for your section in this book.

I want to thank my wonderful son Timothy for the inspiration that ignited my personal transformation. This book has been written from a place of love and a passion to serve others. It wasn't a straight line but instead there were many ups and downs, with periodic moments of negative self-talk, but ultimately followed by passion and excitement.

The five Pillars in this book are what enabled me to see this project to completion and to appreciate the contrast along the way. I welcomed the support of my family, friends and my inspiring network to keep me on track.

I am also very happy to give a special shout out to the following:

Simone Graham, my editor and friend. Your intuitive skills, passion, work ethic and positive energy really kept me moving forward. This book would not have been possible without your powerful and heartfelt contribution.

Carolyn McNall, my graphic designer and friend. You continued to over-deliver with everything from my logo design and website through to the book design. Keep rocking what you do.

Patrick Doyle, my brother. Thank you for inspiring me through the amazing growth of your own company and for the section you wrote in this book. Your confidence, vision and ability to create the things you seek will continue to keep me motivated to be moving forward.

Sharon LeShane, my sister. Thank you for believing in me and supporting me. From playing a major role when I first got into the field of finance to encouraging me when I took up running, thank you for always being there.

Maureen (Mo) Hagan. Thank you for your contribution to this book as well as your ongoing support. I am grateful for our friendship and honoured you are a part of my journey. You are a true inspiration!

Sara Ivanisevic and Jakob Fowler of Old East Village Fitness. Thank you for your ongoing contribution toward my personal growth. Having Sara as my personal trainer enabled me to not only add lean muscle but grow in other areas of my life. Sara, I want you to know that your positive energy and passion for fitness is contagious.

Melissa Schenk. I am grateful for our friendship, your amazing energy and ongoing support. Your advice on my videos and branding is truly appreciated. MS2 Productions are top of the charts and I am excited for where our work together will lead us.

Gerry Visca (Why Guy) and Angela Kontgen (Mindfulness Guru). Thank you for all your support and inspiring publications.

Elias Puurunen. Thank you for your friendship, motivating brainstorming sessions, many coffee meet- ups, and top notch IM/IT support. Excited to see where you bring Tractus and business ventures to in 2023 and beyond.

Stuart Crose. Thank you for your meaningful friendship and encouragement. You have been there through the peaks and valleys and always have a solid caring support for me. Love picking tunes with you and look forward to many more tunes in the future.

In closing, I am very happy to dedicate this book to my parents, Patrick and Mary Doyle.

Thank you!

ABOUT THE AUTHOR

Michael Doyle is a peak performance and leadership expert, a best-selling author, a gifted speaker, and an intuitive coach. He has an innate ability to unlock the potential in others, so they can follow their dreams and fulfill the deeper purpose of their lives. Michael's process is powerful, and it works. Taking a common-sense approach, he can effectively motivate, influence, and guide companies and their teams to work in a "collective flow."

Having transformed his own life from being exhausted, overweight and stuck, to the point where he is now thriving, is living proof his programs, systems, and approaches are very effective. Peaceful, strong, and happy, Michael draws on his natural gifts of humour, intuition, and life experiences to help bring out the full potential in the people and businesses who engage with him.

He has a passion for Canada's Arctic, with more than 20 years of extensive experience working with clients, companies, and Government organizations in Nunavut. Living now in London, Ontario with his son, Michael lives his life in alignment and joy. He invites you to go after the freedom that comes with taking charge of your life.

Doyle It In Mantras

Decide your path.

Organize your plan.

You are in control.

Learn to receive from others.

Elevate the people around you.

Increase your productivity.

Take time to be still daily.

Invest into your personal growth.

Never stop believing.

~ Michael Doyle

Printed in the United States
by Baker & Taylor Publisher Services